Citizen City

CITIZEN CITY

Vancouver's Henriquez Partners Challenges Architects to Engage
in Partnerships that Advance Cultural Sustainability

MARYA COTTEN GOULD | GREGORY HENRIQUEZ | ROBERT ENRIGHT

BLUEiMPRINT

BLUEIMPRINT
5525 West Blvd, Suite 501
Vancouver, BC Canada V6M 3W6

Cataloguing data available from Library and Archives Canada
ISBN 978-1-897476-80-2 (pbk.)
ISBN 978-1-77229-014-1 (ebook)

Editing by Robert Enright
Copy Editing by Elaine Corden
Cover and interior design by Naomi MacDougall
Cover photographs by Colin Goldie
Maps, diagrams & drawings by Arnold Wong
Printed and bound in Korea

All renderings are produced by Henriquez Partners Architects except
for *Creative Energy*, which is provided courtesy of Bjarke Ingels Group,
Copenhagen.

Interior photographs by Ed White except for images on
pages 31, 32, 33 and 35, by Bob Matheson, pages 34 and 38 by
Paul Warchol, and pages 36–37, 39, and 40, by Darryl Humphrey.

The publisher gratefully acknowledges the financial support of the
Canada Council for the Arts, the British Columbia Arts Council, and the
Government of Canada through the Canada Book Fund.

10 9 8 7 6 5 4 3 2 1

for Jacob, Sarita, and Francesco, and the inclusive society we dream of . . .

Preface

GREGORY HENRIQUEZ

Why This Book Now?

THIS SMALL BOOK was born out of my love for the profession of architecture. It is a passion I inherited from my father, whose life work inspired me as a child to follow in his footsteps. I witnessed the power of my father's designs to affect physical change in the urban landscape. His ability to dream, draw, model, and build alternate realities was purely and simply a form of alchemy.

As I developed as a young man and architect, I came to understand the complexity of the field and appreciate the many skills needed to translate intentions into form. The knowledge required to be successful includes not only the art and science of the craft but also an authentic participation in the world of the work. This skill set includes the mastery of business, politics, and the bureaucratic landscape if one were to realize anything of substance beyond conventional practice.

The projects compiled in this book are the culmination of over 25 years of architectural experimentation, which stand firmly with the advantage of being grounded upon the 50 years of my father's practice. The aspiration of the book is to illustrate, through 10 specific projects, the latent potential within the architect's role to not merely be a tool of others, but instead be seen as an activating force in the creation of our cities.

I believe there is a malaise within both the education of the profession and the media's articulation of the role of the architect. We have become the instrument of business and market forces whose ethical compasses can often be uninspired and self-serving. The projects described in this book, which are blessed with rare enlightened clients, are a drop in the ocean, but are a little attempt to take a meaningful role in enabling "the good" within our communities. While all of the projects are located within a few blocks in downtown Vancouver, I believe the lessons they provide are both universal and exportable.

To many pure design oriented architects within our profession, we are seen as "selling out" when we participate in the engine of commerce. I would argue that our role is too essential and too important to relinquish to others. So this is an architecture of resistance, cloaked in convention.

This book is written for young architects who feel they are powerless. What I would say to students of architecture is to learn your craft and dream new paradigms, but also to participate in the communities in which you live. While our communication today seems boundless and global, we still eat, sleep, and procreate as we have for millennia. For true meaning to exist in any artistic endeavour, it must be grounded in both the daily life of humanity and the world of the work. Look around you and ask yourself what you would like to change for the better. Seek out mentors, friends, and colleagues who share your passions.

All revolutions start as grassroots movements.

Introduction

MARYA COTTEN GOULD

What is a Citizen City?

ACCORDING TO THE United Nations, more than half of the world's population today—3.9 billion people—live in urban areas and by 2050, it is estimated that 66 percent of the world's population will be living in cities.[1] Urbanization is a major trend of the 21st century and is a fundamental component in achieving sustainable development as the world's population grows exponentially and the resources of our planet are increasingly constrained. When cities are operating in their ideal sense, they can serve as hubs for commerce, job development, and economic growth, as well as centres for innovation, culture, and community.

The vision of a Citizen City is one that transcends the traditional urban goals of economic stability and working infrastructure, and allows for inclusivity of its people, with a variety of economic levels, different cultures, and diverse identities. A Citizen City also provides and encourages open access to democratic and civic engagement, and develops cultural facilities and promotes cultural identity, thus enhancing a sense of community. Diversity, inclusivity, and civic engagement represent the true "richness" of an urban center and can provide the basis for cultural sustainability: this is a Citizen City.

In *The Just City*, Susan Fainstein champions the concept of a "just city" as an approach to moral urban planning and development that incorporates three central concepts in her conception of justice: equity, democracy, and diversity.[2] She explains why she prefers the term "equity" over "equality":

> [T]he goal of equality is too complex, demanding, and unrealistic to be an objective in the context of capitalist cities. It acts as a magnet for all the objections based on rewards to the most deserving, on questions of the obliteration of incentives, on the trade-off between growth and equality, and on the unfairness of penalizing everyone above the median in the name of the greater good.[3]

Equity, Fainstein argues, is a term that connotes fairness, which is a broader-appealing and less inflammatory term politically than equality. Fairness is more achievable normative value to be striving for in urban planning, particularly in a North American market economy. According to Fainstein, equity "refers to a distribution of both material and nonmaterial benefits derived from public policy that does not favor those already better off at the beginning."[4] This means that the disadvantaged should be taken into account in making urban planning decisions as a form of redistributive justice. Making public policy decisions from a pro-equity standpoint means that outcomes of those decisions should be evaluated in accordance with the distribution of those benefits. A simple example would be allocating funding for the improvement of a community centre in a traditionally underserved neighbourhood instead of one in a neighbourhood that already has a myriad of recreational and cultural opportunities.

Democracy in its best public policy sense means participation in a process that is deliberative, participatory, and open. In the urban planning process, this is often meant to include citizen participation in the decision-making process as a way of ensuring that the politicians and bureaucrats making decisions are informed as to the opinions and interests of the residents who will be impacted by these decisions. Particularly in the 1960s and 1970s, the call for "community control" became a rallying cry for urban activists. The need for community input is particularly urgent if the decision-makers are perceived to be from a "sharply different social strata from those affected by their decisions."[5] Including the communities in the process by which decisions are made is a laudable public policy goal, but is often still criticized on the basis that it becomes a way to further middle-class interests while neglecting those of the poor. In addition, minority communities of any composition do not have monolithic viewpoints, and community activists may not always represent the interests of the community more broadly, but rather may represent a tiny but vocal minority of interests.[6] In general, however, institutionalizing the pathways for community participation promotes more open and democratic decision-making, and can result in more knowledgeable government decision-making by providing urban policy makers with a sense of community interests.[7]

Diversity can be a tricky term in any context, and this complexity is not alleviated in the context of urban planning. However, as Fainstein notes, "Diversity . . . is convenient shorthand, encompasses reference to the physical environment as well as social relations, and refers to policy ambitions that go beyond encouraging acceptance of others to include the social composition of places."[8] That is to say, diversity should include both diversity in the use of physical space, and the diversity of the social mix found in these places. Diversity in the urban context should be construed as broadly as possible. A true Citizen City includes welcoming diversity in race and ethnic background, religion, income levels, physical ability, age, size and composition of households, and sexual identity and orientation.

"Inclusivity" provides a descriptive umbrella for encompassing all of these laudable values in a normative vision of urban planning in providing equity by including all urban inhabitants in the vision of—and ability to live in—a Citizen City. Inclusivity must be integrated with the democratic process, and represent individuals within that process while welcoming diversity of all kinds by insisting on inclusivity in urban communities and spaces. Furthermore, this inclusivity naturally creates a more just and vibrant city that can lead to greater social and cultural sustainability.

Sustainability is a broad term that has evolved over time to include social and cultural sustainability. An oft-cited definition of sustainable development is "development that meets the needs of the present without compromising the ability of future generations to meet their own needs." This definition emerged as part of the United Nations' 1987 Brundtland Report.[9] The definition inherently contains the pressing need for environmental sustainability but the report also discusses social imperatives like health and poverty reduction. By 1992, at the World Commission on Environment and Development meeting, the concept of social sustainability was expanded by discussions of components like social justice, local participation in development, healthy environment, safety, and access to education.[10] Cultural sustainability is a more recently added pillar to the larger sustainability discussion and is largely viewed as an extension of social sustainability. It is typically thought to include access to—and preservation of—cultural resources, recognition of cultural heritage including human-built objects, and such abstract qualities as creativity and "a sense of place."[11] Ideally, cultural sustainability should include cultural vitality and diversity, cultural landscape and heritage, and cultural creation, access, and participation.

Engaging all sectors of society in working towards a more inclusive city that generates cultural vitality and access as well as a feeling of community and a "sense of place" is the objective of a Citizen City.

Canadian Values as a Context for a Citizen City

Our conception of a Citizen City is rooted in Western culture; specifically, our discussion focusses on Vancouver, Canada. "Western culture" is no longer merely a geographic designation of Europe, but rather a shorthand way to refer to traditional European political and cultural underpinnings in Europe, as well as areas of the globe impacted by large-scale European migration such as North and South America. The hallmark of enlightened Western cultures is a liberal democracy, with free and fair elections resulting in representative democracy. While democratic rule favors the majority, liberal democracies also have inherent protections of human rights that value individuals and minorities. There is an emphasis on open and transparent government as well as the rule of law. This rule of law provides stability and predictability that serves as an essential platform for a mixed-market economy in which the private sector and varying levels of government direct the economy. There are also social norms and ethics that have developed as a result of the shared political, economic, cultural, and religious history.

While most Western democracies have similar values and cultural underpinnings, it is important to highlight the cultural values as they present themselves as uniquely Canadian. Canada is primarily a parliamentary democracy with a federal bicameral legislature comprised of the Senate, made up of members appointed by the Governor General to represent the 10 provinces and three territories, as well as an elected House of Commons. Canada is also a constitutional monarchy, although while government acts are executed in the name of the Crown (the current Queen of the United Kingdom as well as the commonwealth nations), it is considered that this authority derives from the power of the Canadian people.[12] Since the Constitution Act of 1982, Canada has achieved, for all practical purposes, full political independence from the United Kingdom. Canada has a federalist system with shared lawmaking authority among the federal government located in Ottawa, and the governments of the provinces and territories. While not without critiques like any country, the political system in Canada is viewed internally and externally at the global level as a stable and successfully functioning one.

Like most liberal democracies, there are legal protections for individuals, particularly those in political and cultural minorities. The Canadian Charter of Rights and Freedoms (the "Charter"), enacted as part of the Constitution Act of 1982, affords Canadian citizens fundamental freedoms like that of expression and religion, democratic rights like voting, mobility rights outside and within Canada, legal rights like procedural protections when accused of a crime, and equality rights like equal protection under the law. This equal protection under the law guards against governmental discrimination based on race, colour, national or ethnic origin, religion, sex, age, or mental or physical disability. The Charter also protects the French-speaking minority. In an explicit acknowledgement of Canada's diversity, the Charter provides that it "shall be interpreted in a manner consistent with the preservation and enhancement of the multicultural heritage of Canadians."[13]

Further federal legislation—the Canadian Human Rights Act of 1977—protects against discrimination by the federal or First Nations governments in employment or receiving services, as well as employment by private companies. The protected classes are broad ones (particularly when compared to federal employment discrimination policies in the United States, for example): race, national or ethnic origin, colour, religion, age, sex, sexual orientation, marital status, family status, disability, and conviction status (if a pardon was granted or the record suspended). There are also provincial and territorial governmental protections against discrimination in workplaces, public accommodations, schools, and housing.

The expansive protection for minorities of all kinds and the emphasis on multiculturalism promotes inclusivity and diversity as Canadian values. The home page for the Canadian Human Rights Commission's website declares simply and proudly, "My Canada includes everyone."[14] This idea of an inclusive Canada, while honouring its diverse cultural constituents, is captured in the metaphor of the "cultural mosaic" so often used to describe Canadian society.[15] This frequently used metaphor is viewed as being a distinct characteristic of Canadian society and a differentiating point between the culture of Canada and its neighbour to the south, the United States. An analogous metaphor used in the United States is the "melting pot." The difference is readily apparent: the mosaic is viewed as a vibrant patchwork of cultures that honours diverse traditions that remain distinct, whereas the melting pot is viewed as an emphasis on assimilation instead of cultural retention and a belief that immigrants, upon arriving in the United States, should shed their customs from their land of origin in favour of the values and customs of their new homeland.

Multiculturalism is more often viewed as an advantage in Canada. As one academic argued,

> Multiculturalism strengthens the Canadian political, economic and social system. Multiculturalism has given Canada a reputation and an international image that we are in the vanguard of acknowledging and managing a national and global reality where cultural diversity is flourishing.[16]

Another value of Canadian society is the belief that each individual deserves a basic standard of living and well-being. This value translates into the existence of universal health care, a social safety net that helps protect the unemployed, seniors, and other vulnerable people, along with a broad understanding among Canadians as to what infrastructure and services are to be provided to Canadians by their federal, provincial (or territorial), and municipal governments. This is not to say that there are not homeless Canadians or challenges with regard to affordable housing for families or seniors and other vulnerable people (see "Challenges in Vancouver" starting on page 19 for more of a discussion on these issues)—as in all nets, there are holes. Like any system, Canada's social safety net is not perfect. However, the existing values in place in Canadian society as a whole make progress on these perceived deficiencies possible and are a compelling part of the mission in striving towards a Citizen City.

In May 2014, *The New York Times* columnist Nicholas Kristof penned an opinion piece entitled, "It's Now the Canadian Dream." The title was a play on historian James Truslow Adams' phrase, "the American dream" which has been used to describe the idea that American life affords individuals the opportunity and ability to be upwardly mobile and to overcome social class. Kristof noted that, with growing inequality of income in the United States, the ability for individuals to achieve upward mobility is better in Canada or Europe.[17] Another report in *The New York Times* noted that while the wealthiest Americans are still wealthier than the wealthy in many other nations, the United States is now lagging behind other nations in other measures. As of 2014, the after-tax middle-class incomes in Canada are higher than those in the United States. In 2010, Americans in the bottom 20 percent of income-earners nationwide had on average 15 percent less than their Canadian counterparts.[18] Canadians enjoy less income inequality and greater economic inclusivity than their American neighbours.

For such a geographically large country, Canada is surprisingly urbanized. More than a third of the Canadian population lives in Montreal, Toronto, or Vancouver.[19] Having a strong and stable democratic system and economy, with a rich political and cultural history of inclusivity and diversity, Canadian society provides a stable foundation upon which the idealistic vision of a Citizen City can flourish. The challenge becomes how to enhance these pre-existing Canadian values by challenging them to operate and, in their best normative sense, be applied in a concrete and practical way to the specific task of creating culturally vibrant and inclusive cities.

Can Vancouver be a Citizen City?

Any mention of Vancouver, Canada inevitably describes the astounding natural beauty of its setting. Downtown Vancouver is situated on a peninsula and features a view of the North Shore Mountains to the north across Burrard Inlet, Stanley Park and English Bay to the west, False Creek and English Bay to the south, with neighbourhoods extending east. The City of Vancouver's overall southern boundary is the Fraser River. The natural geography of the Vancouver area, as well as the 49th parallel (the border with the United States to the south), limits the ability for urban sprawl, and also drives the rate of densification of the greater metropolitan area, known as Metro Vancouver (and formerly known as the Greater Vancouver Regional District).[20] The built area of Vancouver's downtown peninsula is relatively small. It would take 12 downtown Vancouvers to equal Manhattan.[21] The population is relatively small as well: in 2011, the City of Vancouver had roughly 600,000 residents and the larger census metropolitan area had approximately 2.3 million residents.[22]

The abundance of water and mountains in all directions from Vancouver's downtown core has created what has been referred to as the "cult of the view."[23] Lance Berelowitz describes this phenomenon in his 2005 book, *Dream City: Vancouver and the Global Imagination*:

> The willingness to pay for spectacular views over the heads of the rest of the city to the sea and mountains beyond is what offsets construction inefficiencies. People have always been drawn to Vancouver for its superb setting, waterfront location and seductive (relative to the rest of Canada) climate. Those endless sunsets (when it's not raining) over the Strait of Georgia sell the units that have views of them, and never more so than now. Buyers, increasingly from offshore or other—landlocked— Canadian provinces, are prepared to pay dearly for their piece of visual paradise.[24]

The desire to buy in Vancouver is not an aesthetic decision alone. It is viewed as a stable place where it is safe to invest. The relative stability of the Canadian economy and the desirability of living in Vancouver make its real estate attractive to investors as well as residents and prospective immigrants.

Vancouver consistently ranks near the top of liveability surveys due to its natural beauty and access to recreational opportunities, its healthcare and educational resources, its stability and safety, and its focus on thoughtful urban planning and infrastructure. In August 2013, The Economist Intelligence Unit released its Global Liveability Ranking and Report with Vancouver ranked as the third most liveable city in the world.[25] It had been in the top five for the previous three years, and prior to that, ranked first.[26] (Canada does well in these surveys in general; Toronto and Calgary were also in the top ten in 2013.)[27]

When incorporated in 1886, the City of Vancouver, situated on a waterway, was primarily a logging town, but by the end of that same year, it had become the terminus of the Canadian Pacific Railway's transcontinental line.[28] Thus Vancouver is a relatively new city, even by North American standards, and it has a continual feel of newness due to the changing demographics from immigration. In 2011, the national census revealed that 40 percent of the population in Metro Vancouver were immigrants. This was substantially higher than the national rate of 21 percent. Furthermore, 32 percent of Metro Vancouver's immigrant population arrived in the decade preceding 2011. Two-thirds of the foreign-born residents in Metro Vancouver are from Asia (including the Middle East).[29] These immigrants to Canada tend to be well-educated. In 2006, more than half of those immigrating to Canada had a college degree, and almost half of Canadians who held a PhD were foreign-born.[30] The economic and political stability of Canada and its perceived opportunities help Canada attract migrants. Being a very safe and pleasant place to live with a mild climate helps Vancouver attract a large proportion of these talented migrants.

Vancouver's urban planning philosophy, which has come to be known around the world as "Vancouverism," has also created a laudable urban setting that has been applauded, studied, and emulated by many west coast cities in North America and around the world. One scholar says Vancouverism is "defined by open spaces, tall slender skyscrapers that afford ample views, and plenty of public transportation."[31] In the words of *The New York Times*, "Vancouverism is characterized by tall, but widely separated, slender towers interspersed with low-rise buildings, public spaces, small parks and pedestrian-friendly streetscapes and facades to minimize the impact of a high-density population."[32] Vancouverism is also an ethos that emphasizes mixed-use development "and the inclusion of community amentities as a part of new developments" in order to provide the services a community needs.

Vancouverism is an urbanism created by architects, developers and urban planners in accordance with a normative standard of a dense but attractive and livable city. Architect Arthur Erickson is often referred to as the father of Vancouverism, and his 1955 *Plan 56* "remains a stunning vision of a high-rise city, where buildings are not massed together as in New York, but elegantly arranged in an undulating cascade that complements the city's natural beauty."[33] When Erickson died, his obituary in *The Globe and Mail* described him as "the greatest architect we ever produced."[34]

Vancouverism has been supported by urban planning decisions and policies that help make Vancouver an attractive place to live. (For a brief overview of the current urban planning mechanisms and policies in place that support Vancouverism, see the sidebar discussion "Urban Planning and Development in Vancouver" on page 41). This liveability, as well as the appeal of Vancouver and Canada to domestic and global investors, has created tremendous demand for real estate in the city. Real estate in Vancouver is an obsession for many. In *City of Glass*, hometown novelist and cultural commentator Douglas Coupland describes real estate as Vancouver's "biggest sport," which is "disturbingly central to the civic psyche."[35] The upside to a real estate market that is attractive to many is that the city attracts enormous levels of investment. The downside is the result that Vancouver is the most expensive city in Canada according to Mercer's 2013 Cost of Living Survey.[36] As one Harvard economist has noted, "The market works, more or less, and when a city has really high housing prices relative to incomes, you can bet that there is something nice about the place."[37]

There are many reasons that Vancouver is popular with residents, tourists, and investors alike. The vibrant multicultural makeup of Vancouver, the city's real estate serving as a global commodity, and the intense focus—both internally and externally—on the City of Vancouver's forward-looking urban planning processes, make Vancouver an interesting laboratory for a Citizen City. As described in more detail starting on page 18, the tremendous wealth—and wealth disparity—in Vancouver create both challenges and opportunities in achieving a Citizen City.

Role of an Architect in Creating a Citizen City

"To take a leading role in contemporary issues, the architect of the 21st century must be a social activist, a realist, a poet, a political technician and a utopian."
—ALBERTO PÉREZ-GÓMEZ [38]

Like any profession or art form, architecture has mutated over time as society itself shifts and is altered by the forces of history. What role does a contemporary architect typically play in society and, does this traditional role promote the creation of a Citizen City? In the classical sense, architecture was viewed as a singular form of poetic beauty and a solid representation of ethical human action. The school of "ethical architecture" posits that this unification of poetics and ethics has been lost over time, and that architects today need to recover the idea that the aesthetics of a building should not be separate from the ethics of the project, and should contain an element of social justice by orienting the project within the community where it is located.[39] This social justice element can be encapsulated by an architect taking a leading role in tackling the collective challenges that exist within a city and offering creative solutions that help address structural societal inequity, the human need for inclusion and safe shelter, and spaces that celebrate daily living, relationships, culture, and community.

In contemporary society, there are many archetypes of architects. There are the "starchitects" who have achieved critical acclaim through numerous awards and a certain level of name recognition, even outside the field: for example, Rem Koolhaas, Frank Gehry, and Santiago Calatrava. They are often courted for big developments or cultural institutions in the hopes that producing an "iconic" building or structure will help with fundraising for the cultural institution or attract people to the building or city. In this way, the architect has become an artistic commodity and the perceived consumption of this commodity as an economic good to be valued. These developments typically emphasize a starchitect's brand of architecture more than providing any context for the city or community where the building is located. The emphasis is on the immediate visual and aesthetic impact, described sometimes as the "wow factor." These architects tend to have a more formalistic orientation, as opposed to a humanistic one. Often aesthetics are prized above function or the impact of the design on the inhabitants of the building. While the career trajectory of starchitects is not representative of most architects, all architects are similar in one profound way: they are still essentially focussed on producing a project for a client.

Architects can be artists, but as professionals they also run businesses and serve clients. Serving client interests is the reality of any service provider. However, ethical architecture prompts architects to remember that they still have independent professional judgment and an ethical duty to consider the interests of the public at large, not just the private interests paying the bills. Even within the client relationship, there is room for the architect's judgment to be employed in exercising his or her professional talents. In an illustration of how ethical decisions can be made by architects that impact the community even within political and economic realities, Canadian philosopher Maurice Lagueux offers this example:

> Should libraries be conceived of as austere temples devoted only to scholarly research or be designed to be attractive as possible in order to incite people of any educational background to use them?... The abstract decision as to whether a library should be open to the general public or to scholars concerns librarians, civil servants and politicians; but the decision as to whether such or such a shape or partitioning of spaces is aesthetically attractive in a way that satisfies the ethically oriented demands of one or more types of users is an architectural decision. One might even say that a solution that, while complying with the structural, functional and other requirements, attracts through aesthetical means as many types of users as possible is a solution that bears the mark of a great architectural achievement.[40]

This supports the idea that architects have a moral imperative to consider the lives of the community the building serves along with the community in which the building exists and to view this community as broadly and inclusively as possible. Architectural achievement should be measured by more than aesthetics alone, and aesthetics can be thoughtfully employed to help implement the ethical. The building's end users should be thought of as a stakeholder and, in many ways, effectively a client, even if they're not paying the bills. As Alberto Pérez-Gómez of the School of Architecture at McGill University has written,

> In other words, good architecture offers societies a place for existential orientation. It allows for participation in meaningful action, conveying to the participant an understanding of his or her place in the world. Successful architecture opens up a clearing for an individual's experience of purpose through participation in cultural institutions.[41]

The creation of a sense of place and cultural engagement through architecture are critical in achieving cultural sustainability in a Citizen City.

In addition to exercising their independent ethical judgment and considering public interest as well as the private interests of the client, architects can serve as facilitators of relationships. The development of relationships among all sectors, such as private developers, government agencies, and community organizations, allows the architect to build a credible reputation that can be employed to encourage the consideration of a broader spectrum of societal interests in his or her projects. While not every goal can be achieved in every project, most projects have elements that allow for the encouragement of strategies to achieve greater urban inclusivity. The case studies highlighted in this book are examples of how projects that employ cooperation among various actors of civil society can achieve gains in urban inclusivity and community enhancement, especially if relationships are strong or a respected part of the development process.

In the course of an architect's career, with the proper focus and energy placed on developing relationships (or becoming a "political technician"), the architect can develop a solid reputation for integrity and having relationships that help facilitate getting projects completed. It is at this point where an architect has the social or political capital to become a thought leader and to help generate proposals and societal solutions, instead of simply responding to requests for proposals. Being an active citizen, in addition to being an architect, results in "citizen architects," who "participate in the social, political, and environmental realities our communities are facing."[42]

As Gregory Henriquez explained in an interview with *Canadian Architect*:

> Some people have been calling me a bit of an activist, but I look at this as a challenge to the community. Everybody does different things in their practices, and we receive incredible education as architects, and thus have more opportunities than to just become service providers. . . . We have to broaden our role and encourage more architects to do the same, to ensure that there is no distinction and specialization, that we are only part of the process. It's essential that the community experiences the poetic, the beautiful and the ethical.[43]

In viewing oneself as a facilitator of relationships and a problem-solver, the contemporary architect is poised to take a leadership role in infusing projects with a melding of the poetic and the ethical. If coming from a standpoint that the ethical is as important as the poetic beauty that can be achieved through architecture, the architect is well-positioned to play a critical leadership role in developing a Citizen City.

Citizen City Challenges and Opportunities in Vancouver

CITIES INHERENTLY have challenges in trying to achieve economic prosperity and create jobs, and provide safety and essential services. This must be provided in the context of constrained resources and desires to minimize environmental impact, battle congestion, address shortages of adequate housing, and deal with infrastructure falling into disrepair. Vancouver, like most cities, has these challenges. Likewise, sustainability is a major concern for Vancouverites as it is for all denizens of Planet Earth. The City of Vancouver has tackled this issue head-on with its Greenest City 2020 Action Plan, and has made major strides in achieving greater sustainability. At the time this plan was unveiled, Vancouver residents had a per capita carbon footprint three times greater than a level that would achieve environmental sustainability, even though the city already had the lowest per capita carbon footprint of any North American city.[44]

While environmental sustainability is an important and urgent issue, the focus here is specifically the pressing challenges facing Vancouver that create the biggest threats to achieving an inclusive and culturally vibrant, community-oriented Citizen City: affordability of housing, and the sociological trends and mindsets that challenge inclusivity and shared community. There are opportunities to tap the incredible wealth in the real estate community in Vancouver and to employ the resources and strengths of all sectors to combat these challenges and work towards achieving a Citizen City.

Challenges in Vancouver

HOUSING AFFORDABILITY & HOMELESSNESS

A 2011 article in *Maclean's* about Vancouver questioned, "The most liveable city?" and highlighted the affordability crisis in Vancouver.[45] To illustrate the discrepancy between incomes and housing prices, consider that according to the 2011 census, the regional Vancouver median income was $68,970.[46] However, in December 2013, the average detached home sales price for the region according to the Real Estate Board of Greater Vancouver was $927,000.[47] The prices for detached single family homes within the city of Vancouver limits are even higher.

The high prices of Vancouver's real estate is a simple mechanism of supply and demand, and demand is high due to the desirability of living in Vancouver and the interest in investing in its real estate by buyers from all over the world, often where the prices in Vancouver are less expensive relative to their place of origin. For example, Vancouver's price to income ratio is one-third of that of Beijing or Shanghai.[48] One New York-based real estate consultant said, "High net worth individuals look at real estate today not as a place to live, but as an investment. It's more stable than currency, bonds or stocks. And there are only a handful of cities around the globe where they invest: London, Hong

Kong, Singapore and New York."[49] While Vancouver is smaller than those cities, it deserves to be added to the list as its real estate is increasingly viewed as a global commodity.

An article in *Vancouver Magazine* suggested that Vancouver is only unaffordable from a North American perspective and not a global one. Vancouver is half as expensive as Moscow, London, Tokyo, or Paris, and on par with similarly situated "most liveable cities" such as Melbourne, Stockholm, and Barcelona. Vancouver's affordability problem, the article's author argued, is putting it into the proper context, and the solution is thinking more like a European: renting, not buying; co-owning; and smaller living spaces.[50]

Whether or not Vancouver is "affordable" on a global scale, it does not alleviate the reality of the high cost of living for those whose incomes are dependent on working in the city and the result that the high prices of real estate create an unachievable goal of home ownership for most people. This has a ripple effect, as many of those working in Vancouver find themselves living increasingly farther from their workplaces, while stretching themselves to buy a home. This increases congestion, creates a larger carbon footprint, and also can be detrimental from a sociological perspective when community support workers like police officers, fire personnel, nurses, teachers, and government workers cannot afford to live in the neighbourhoods they serve. Many young people find themselves opting out of living in Vancouver for a more affordable location, which results in a brain drain of talent and culture. Many argue that Vancouver is not so unaffordable if one looks to rent instead of buy, but this ignores the traditional wealth-building mechanism that home ownership provides and has the effect of a widening disparity of wealth between those who rent and those who can afford to buy. This is magnified when one views the disparity through an inter-generational lens—younger generations will be unable to accumulate wealth through home ownership as their parents and grandparents did.

The relative affordability of renting compared with owning is often used to refute the claim that Vancouver is in danger of becoming a luxury resort town for the rich. This claim is also often leveled at New York City and London, both of which are cities without the same differential in the rental versus ownership costs as Vancouver. Part of this discrepancy in Vancouver is due to the fact that so many owners in Vancouver are investors, not inhabitants, and thus there is a bolstering of the supply of rental stock that keeps prices lower than they otherwise would be. (Although rental rates of investor-owned condominiums tend to be higher than purpose-built rentals and the steadiness of the supply is questionable since investors can decide to sell at any time.) Additionally, the rental vacancy rates in Vancouver are still quite low, averaging just 0.9 percent over the past 30 years.[51] The City of Vancouver has created incentive programs to encourage developers to build more rental housing as part of its strategy to increase affordable options for Vancouverites. This is part of the City's plan to protect existing rental stock, diversify rental stock, and encourage the development of purpose-built rentals in order to strive towards greater affordability. For a discussion on the different types of housing available in Vancouver, see the sidebar discussion on The Housing Continuum on page 45.

Under the leadership of Mayor Gregor Robertson, the City of Vancouver is focussing on the need for affordable housing because the situation is particularly challenging in a city where real estate is a commodity. Within the City of Vancouver, nearly 40 percent of households spend more than 30 percent of their gross income on housing.[52] The cost of housing renders many people vulnerable and results in more homelessness or people living with the threat of homelessness. For example, Metro Vancouver considers people at risk for homelessness if they are spending at least half of their current income on their housing. The latest statistic the agency has reported, based on the 2006 census, states that seven percent of the households across Metro Vancouver (55,765 of 757,900 households) were in this category.[53]

Homelessness is a serious problem in Vancouver due to cost of housing as well as other societal challenges like mental illness and substance abuse. (For a fuller discussion on homelessness in Vancouver, see the sidebar, "The Downtown Eastside and Homelessness in Vancouver" on page 47). The issue of homelessness is exacerbated by the pressures of development, which can result in gentrification and displacement. As described in "The Downtown Eastside and Homelessness in Vancouver," tackling the issue of homelessness has become a top priority for the City of Vancouver and is a critical obstacle to overcome if Vancouver is to become a true Citizen City.

NEED FOR INTEGRATION & RESISTANCE TO CHANGE

As described earlier, the demographics of Vancouver are constantly evolving. However, economic integration of immigrants is a trickier issue. For example, in the province of British Columbia, immigrants continue to earn less than their Canadian-born counterparts; this is true regardless of level of education or gender.[54] In Vancouver, immigrants earn approximately two-thirds of what the City's Canadian-born population does, even if they have a university degree.[55] The rates of unemployment are also higher for immigrants. In 2011, for example, the unemployment rate for recent immigrants to Canada was 19.4 percentage points greater than the unemployment rate of the Canadian-born population.[56]

In addition to the challenge of fully integrating immigrants into the economy, there is also the challenge of nation-building. While the Canadian mosaic proudly recognizes the uniqueness of varying cultural backgrounds, there is still a question of how to integrate society culturally and create a sense of community and shared values. This becomes increasingly important since the 21st century has revealed a trajectory for a growing separation of caucasians and visible minorities in Vancouver to each choose to live in areas where they represent a majority. In fact, Daniel Hiebert, a professor at University of British Columbia, has studied this trajectory and by extrapolation suggests the degree of separation between caucasians and visible minorities in Vancouver will begin to approach the separation of caucasians and African-Americans in the average city in the United States in 2010.[57] This portends the need for increased inclusivity and social and economic integration of immigrants in Vancouver if it is indeed to become a Citizen City with a sense of inclusion and community that is culturally sustainable.

Another challenge facing Vancouver is that the changing demographics have increased the need for density. Increased density, along with the rate of development make it a constantly evolving city. There is an ongoing tension between preservation of the status quo and an emphasis on history on one hand, and new development and the inevitable tides of change on the other hand. While the capacity for urban change could be viewed as a strength for Vancouver, it has created—particularly in certain neighbourhoods—a resistance to change and a differential between neighbourhoods that have experienced change and continue to accept it, and entrenchment in areas that have not seen as much and therefore resist change. This can also create an obstacle to achieving a Citizen City if certain parts of the city are expected to bear the brunt of urban evolution and growth, while other swaths of the city resist increased densification. Densification will be an imperative due to a growing population as well as the City of Vancouver's ambitious plan towards a lower carbon footprint and greater overall sustainability, which will require more density in public-transit-oriented neighbourhoods.

There are also many new projects, like social housing or new infrastructure, that suffer from NIMBYism: opposition based on the perception of possible detrimental impacts on one's own property values, or the desirability or safety of the immediate neighbourhood.[58] Inequity in bearing urban burdens and in receiving an allocation of resources will result in the failure to achieve inclusivity and a true community.

Opportunities Presented in Vancouver

While the affordability crisis and Vancouver's homeless population highlight the wealth disparity in the city, the tremendous wealth that exists in Vancouver has the potential to be channeled and utilized to help make Vancouver a more inclusive city for all of its residents as well as culturally sustainable. One way of achieving this is prioritizing development of projects that generate more affordable housing, or provide cultural amenities or allocate resources to traditionally underserved or vulnerable populations. This can be a measurable and achievable step towards true inclusion.

Regulation and public policy are the primary ways that the public sector ensures a private sector contribution to community needs. In Vancouver, one such mechanism in the urban planning process is the Community Amenity Contribution (which is described in more detail in the "Urban Planning and Development in Vancouver" sidebar on page 41). By tapping the wealth creation within the development process itself, the City of Vancouver can ensure that a portion of this wealth is reallocated to the community or the city at large, by using the developer's contribution to build social housing, parks, daycares, cultural facilities, and other amenities. This helps generate the mixed-use, pedestrian-oriented developments the city is famed for worldwide. The Community Amenity Contribution is essentially a government policy that requires a wealth transfer from the private sector to the community at large. This mechanism in many ways can only work—at least at this magnitude—in a city where real estate commands top dollar.

In general, government bodies have the ability to regulate and to set policy priorities, and must serve their respective constituents. They are subject to the political process and often have resource constraints in terms of time, staffing, and funding. The private sector is not subject to the same bureaucratic processes and procurement rules that are the hallmarks of government action, and thus, has more flexibility and can more nimbly act. The private sector is also not typically subject to the resource constraints that the government may have, and its wealth creates the ability to take more risks and to experiment more. The downside is the private sector is, by definition, more profit focussed and may not have the interest in engaging in socially valuable endeavors, even though these activities may help attract and retain employees and increase public recognition and visibility.[59] Non-profit organizations have the will and passion to tackle society's difficult problems because they exist for this mission, however, they often are resource constrained. One of their greatest assets, however, can be their credibility and reputation, particularly in the communities and populations they serve. This can be an incredibly important part of the equation, especially when viewed through the lens of accomplishing a cross-sector real estate development or community project.

The opportunity to make strides towards achieving a Citizen City in Vancouver is provided by cooperation among all sectors to solve the city's greatest challenges. The prevailing wisdom in Vancouver seems to be an inherent understanding that all sectors have assets and resources to contribute, and that cooperation, a certain interdependence, and visionary leadership within each sector are necessities if progress is to be made on the city's most pressing problems. Despite the potential of cross-sector collaborations, they can present business and administrative challenges. Each partner can have its own agenda and organizational concerns, the relationships among partners take time to develop, and the partners need to share common goals and not dominate each other. Expectations may need to be tempered as optimism and passion meet up with realism. Each partner also needs committed staff members who are able to build trust with the other partners and serve as point people for implementing the program or project.[60] As the level of commitment required for creative collaboration rises, so does the complexity of skills required by each partner's management in planning, negotiating and managing the project, especially when there can be cross-cultural elements when working with another sector.[61]

Under the right circumstances, however, cross-sector partnerships or collaborations can be a powerful force in implementing positive social change and increasing the inclusivity of a city and its cultural resources. An exemplar of this powerful force of cross-sector collaboration is the perfect storm of circumstances where a multitude of sectors mobilized in Vancouver to successfully create an inclusive real estate development: the Woodward's Redevelopment project.

26

Woodward's Redevelopment and the Children of Woodward's

In 1903, the Woodward's department store opened in what was then the commercial centre of Vancouver, at Hastings and Abbott streets. For decades, people came from all over the region to shop at Woodward's for their household needs. In 1993 the store shuttered after its parent company, Woodward Stores Ltd, went bankrupt, and the Woodward's building at Hastings and Abbott became a symbol of the decline of the area and the shift of the city's downtown core to points west. Over time, an impassioned debate grew around the disused Woodward's space and the future of the Downtown Eastside neighbourhood that surrounded it. An attempted redevelopment of the former Woodward's site in 1995 suffered from vehement opposition and floundered, largely because of the plan's failure to include any plans for social housing. The site sat dormant while protests raged, culminating in the 2002 "Woodsquat" protest staged by community groups and homeless people angry about the inaction at the site and a desire for more social housing in the neighbourhood. Motivated by a desire to control the site's destiny, the City of Vancouver purchased the site from the provincial government the following year, and issued a developer request for proposals in 2004. The selected team, Westbank Projects/Peterson Investment Group, along with Henriquez Partners Architects and community partner Portland Hotel Society, worked with three levels of government—federal, provincial and municipal— and various community groups to build public trust and engagement.

The successful result is an almost 1,000,000-square-foot development. There are 536 market-rate units of housing, 200 units of social housing, community space, a daycare, and commercial space including a drugstore, grocery store, bank, and café. It also houses the Simon Fraser University School for the Contemporary Arts and various government offices for the City of Vancouver and the Canadian Federal Government including the National Film Board of Canada and the Public Health Agency of Canada. In itself, the Woodward's Redevelopment is a prime example of Vancouverism, enlivened with a mix of renovations and decorated with quotations about the history of the Woodward's department store as well as new buildings. It also emulates the inclusivity and cultural sustainability that are the ideals of a Citizen City. In the words of Gregory Henriquez:

> The narrative [of this project] is about inclusivity and humanity's ability to co-exist on all social and economic planes, to not ghettoize ourselves by living behind walls. Woodward's has single-room occupancy housing—which is the poorest of the poor in our society—right across from $1.5 million, sky-balcony, three-level apartments. These people are going to share a common ground plane.[62]

The cross-sector collaboration that achieved the Woodward's Redevelopment project has inspired many of its participants to generate new ideas on how to continue the tide of inclusivity and community building, in some cases, even collaborating with the same partners again. The case studies found in this book are an exploration of cross-sector collaboration in real estate development in Vancouver and the challenges and strengths presented by working with various partners. These projects are in many ways the offspring of the Woodward's Redevelopment project, and represent the civic leadership role Henriquez Partners Architects played.

In an interview by Robert Enright in *Body Heat*, a book about the Woodward's Redevelopment, Gregory Henriquez said of contemporary architects that, "the biggest failing of my profession is the inability to have sufficient faith in itself and in humanity to believe that it can make a difference."[63] The afterword of this book is an interview with Gregory Henriquez by Robert Enright, in the spirit of a "Letter to a Young Architect," in which Henriquez reflects on the personal awakening he felt during the Woodward's Redevelopment project. He challenges the architecture community—particularly fledgling architects—towards greater civic engagement and the assumption of a leadership role in the pursuit of social justice, inclusivity, and cultural sustainability in the cities and communities where they live and work.

← **WOODWARD'S BUILDING**
Located in the 100 block of
West Hastings St. in Vancouver.

Urban Planning and Development in Vancouver

In *The Vancouver Achievement: Urban Planning and Design,* urban design scholar John Punter describes the Vancouver zoning system as a hybrid of a highly discretionary system (like that of the United Kingdom) and an administrative one (more common in Continental Europe and the United States).[64] Typically a site will have a set zoning designation, with an additional discretionary component. It is not unfettered discretion of City officials, because the City's bylaws have some guidelines. However, the system does allow for spot zoning, and planners have the ability to adjust the height, siting, and design of the proposed buildings. For these reasons, Vancouver is typically viewed as having a flexible zoning system, with the benefit that it allows projects perceived to be innovative and beneficial to move forward. Critiques of this type of system generally include the notion that it is time-consuming, can be unpredictable, and vulnerable to favouritism. The size and complexity of a project determines whether a development permit application is reviewed by the Director of Planning, or for larger projects, the Development Permit Board.[65]

Vancouver also has an Urban Design Panel which does not approve or reject projects, but advises City Council and City staff about major development or rezoning proposals, or civic building projects. This is to ensure that urban design is fully considered as part of major projects. The Urban Design Panel consists of a member of the City Planning Commission, several architects, engineers, landscape architects, and a professional artist.[66]

To understand the basics of development in Vancouver, one must understand development cost levies and community amenity contributions (two sets of costs that developers pay for development) as well as density bonus zoning.

41

DEVELOPMENT COST LEVIES (DCLS): In 1990, the Province of British Columbia amended the Vancouver Charter and provided Vancouver City Council with the authority to use DCLs as a method of funding capital expenditures, particularly those needed due to growth or additional development in the city. DCLs funds can be applied to childcare facilities, infrastructure, replacing housing or parks. There are 11 DCL districts throughout Vancouver with varying DCL rates. There is a city-wide DCL, areas with their own DCL rate (in lieu of the city-wide rate), and areas with layered rates (subject to the area-specific rate as well as the city-wide rate). DCL rates also vary based on the type of development. DCLs are applied on a per-square-foot basis and are payable when a building permit is issued. Projects that do not increase square footage, tiny additions, tax-exempt churches and social housing are all exempt. Some affordable housing projects or those which preserve heritage buildings may be exempt from DCLs. There are also a few areas exempt from the city-wide DCL due to municipal policy.[67]

COMMUNITY AMENITY CONTRIBUTIONS (CACS): CACS vary from DCLs in a couple of important aspects. They apply only to projects requiring a rezoning and are due prior to the rezoning enactment. They are considered voluntary because they are not required by law, but in practice rezoning applications do not move forward without a CAC. CACS are not paid on a per-square-foot basis but are usually an amount, negotiated between the City of Vancouver and the developer, that represents a portion of the increased value of the project due to the rezoning.[68] It is intended to offset the impact of increased usage of city facilities by virtue of the rezoning. The usage of the CAC contribution is often also negotiated between the developer and the City. Typical CACS include parks, transportation facilities, childcare facilities, and community or cultural spaces.

CACs are often lauded as providing much needed or desired community amenities. However, a recent report by the provincial government also expresses concern that the costs of CACs may have a potential impact on housing affordability if CACs are a significant cost of development that put upward price pressures on housing.[69]

DENSITY BONUS ZONING: A developer can receive additional density over the base level of zoning if the developer meets certain conditions. In Vancouver, this is either an amenity density bonus through the CAC process or a heritage bonus for preserving heritage sites. Heritage bonus density typically can be used on site, placed in the heritage density bank for sale, or transferred to a receiver site.[70] With heritage bonus density, the current City policy disfavors the transfer of the density generated and it generally requires that the density bonus be used on the generating site. Developers are concerned that there is increasingly no market for the heritage density that is currently in the heritage density bank.

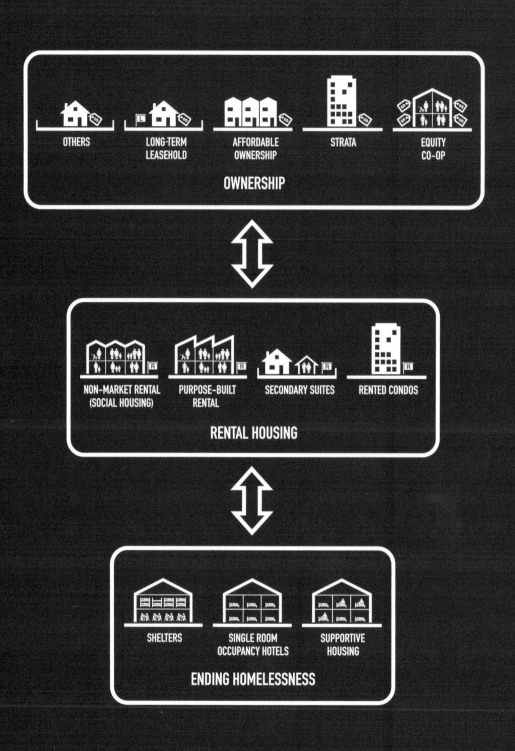

OWNERSHIP

OTHERS · LONG-TERM LEASEHOLD · AFFORDABLE OWNERSHIP · STRATA · EQUITY CO-OP

RENTAL HOUSING

NON-MARKET RENTAL (SOCIAL HOUSING) · PURPOSE-BUILT RENTAL · SECONDARY SUITES · RENTED CONDOS

ENDING HOMELESSNESS

SHELTERS · SINGLE ROOM OCCUPANCY HOTELS · SUPPORTIVE HOUSING

The Housing Continuum

Glossary*

AFFORDABLE HOUSING can be provided by the City, government, non-profit, community and for-profit partners, and can be found or developed along the whole housing continuum including SROs, market rental, and affordable home ownership. The degree of housing affordability results from the relationship between the cost of housing and household income. It is not a static concept, as housing costs and incomes change over time.

EMERGENCY SHELTERS are temporary accommodation for the homeless; they prevent people from becoming street homeless.

SINGLE ROOM OCCUPANCY (SRO) HOUSING is the most affordable form of rental housing provided by the market. In Vancouver, the stock of SROs was built in the early 1900s to provide transitional housing largely for men working in the resource industries. A typical SRO unit is one room of about 10 × 10 feet with shared bathrooms and minimal or no cooking facilities. Over the last 20 years, a significant portion of SROs in the city have been bought and are operated by government or a non-profit partner.

SUPPORTIVE HOUSING is non- market housing (see next definition) that, in addition to rental subsidy to make the housing affordable, also includes ongoing and targeted support services to residents who cannot live independently due to health problems and or other disabilities. This housing type can be provided in congregate settings or in scattered apartments. Typical support services include mental health and or other health supports, life skills training, and meal preparation.

SOCIAL HOUSING/NON-MARKET HOUSING is housing for low and moderate income singles and families, usually subsidized through a variety of mechanisms, including senior government support. The current model in Vancouver is a self-contained unit with private bathroom and kitchen, owned or operated by government or a non-profit. The rents vary to enable a mix of incomes and can range from the value of the shelter component of Income Assistance to 30 percent of tenant's income including market rents.

SECURE MARKET RENTAL/PURPOSE-BUILT RENTAL HOUSING is apartments and/or buildings that are built with the intent to be rented in the private market. Through regulation, they cannot be separated and sold as separate stratas.

SECONDARY SUITES are typically additional units within the structure of a principal single family residence, and are often basement apartments or lock-off suites in townhouses/apartments.

RENTED CONDOMINIUMS are investor-owned condominium (strata) units rented on the private market.

CONDOMINIUMS are buildings in which units of property are owned individually, while the common property is owned jointly by all of the owners.

OTHER OWNERSHIP refers primarily to single family dwellings and row house forms that are not owned as strata properties (i.e. condominiums).

*This Glossary was developed by the City of Vancouver in its report, "Vancouver's Housing and Homeless Strategy 2012-2021"

The Downtown Eastside and Homelessness in Vancouver

The Downtown Eastside of Vancouver (DTES) is often referred to as the poorest postal code in Canada. A 2007 survey by the City of Vancouver found that 67 percent of its residents were low-income, 22 percent were unemployed and at least 40 percent received some form of government transfer payment.[71] As a relatively small neighbourhood of about 18,000 people, it is riddled with crime, drug use, homelessness, mental illness, and communicable diseases.[72] For example, the incidence of HIV infection equals the rates in Botswana, about 30 percent.[73] A study by the Vancouver Police Department revealed that almost half of the emergency calls placed in the neighbourhood were related to mental health issues.[74]

Its population is largely transient and marginalized. This dates back to the 1900s due to the prevalence of low-income single room occupancy (SRO) hotel rooms that rent on a short-term basis.[75] SROs tend to be the most affordable rental housing because the buildings that contain them are often old and in disrepair and simply provide a sleeping room with shared washroom facilities. As owners raise rents or renovate to attract higher-paying customers, the lack of stable housing for low-income people in the DTES leads to even higher rates of homelessness.

Figuring out a city's homeless population is a notoriously difficult and imprecise measure to make. It depends on how you define homelessness and whether homeless people in emergency shelters and those in temporary accommodations like hospitals or relatives' homes are included, or only people sleeping on the street (often called "street homelessness"). On March 12, 2014, a 24 hour homeless count in the Metro Vancouver area was conducted. According to the preliminary count released in April 2014, there were 538 people in the City of Vancouver who spent the night on the street, and another 1,260 people who were in shelters, safe houses, or transitional houses during that same period.[76] The number of street homeless tripled in 2014 from the last count conducted in 2011, which found 154 people.[77] This increase was in spite of aggressive and ambitious efforts by Mayor Gregor Robertson and the Vancouver City Council to end street homelessness by 2015. (According to Mayor Robertson, the 2014 count is still an improvement from the 2008 figure of 811 people who were street homeless during the count.) To address homelessness, the City has invested in emergency winter shelter beds, interim housing, and has made policy moves to prevent unnecessary evictions of people at risk of homelessness.

In a response to the 2014 count, Mayor Robertson addressed the setback in the numbers in *The Vancouver Sun* and identified the closure of some of the temporary shelter housing, construction delays in BC Housing's new supportive housing projects, and the evictions by private landlords who own SRO units. According to the City of Vancouver, 1,700 units of supportive housing have opened since 2010 (439 units in 2014 alone), with more under development, which will help decrease homelessness. The Mayor pledges that the City of Vancouver will continue to advocate for its homeless. As the mayor stated in *The Vancouver Sun*, "In a city with as much wealth, compassion and innovation as Vancouver, there is no reason anyone should have to sleep on the street at night. As mayor, I will ensure the city stays focused on solutions, continue to advocate for new partnerships, and follow through on our plan to end street homelessness."[78]

FOOTNOTES

1   United Nations, Department of Economic and Social Affairs, Population Division (2014).
    World Urbanization Prospects: The 2014 Revision, Highlights (ST/ESA/SER.A/352).
    (For comparison, in 1950 only 30 percent of the global population lived in urban centres.)
2   Fainstein, Susan S. *The Just City*. Ithaca: Cornell University Press, 2010. Print.
3   Fainstein, Susan S. *The Just City*. Ithaca: Cornell University Press, 2010. 36. Print.
4   Fainstein, Susan S. *The Just City*. Ithaca: Cornell University Press, 2010. 36. Print.
5   Fainstein, Susan S. *The Just City*. Ithaca: Cornell University Press, 2010. 64. Print.
6   Fainstein, Susan S. *The Just City*. Ithaca: Cornell University Press, 2010. 66. Print.
7   Corburn, Jason. *Street Science Community Knowledge and Environmental Health Justice*.
    Cambridge, MA: MIT Press, 2005. Print.
8   Fainstein, Susan S. *The Just City*. Ithaca: Cornell University Press, 2010. 67. Print.
9   Brundtland, Gro Harlem. "Report of the World Commission on Environment and
    Development." *Our Common Future*. Oxford University Press (1987) Print.
10 Axelsson, Robert, Per Angelstam, Erik Degerman, Sara Teitelbaum, Kjell Andersson,
    Marine Elbakidze, and Marcus K. Drotz. "Social and Cultural Sustainability: Criteria,
    Indicators, Verifier Variables for Measurement and Maps for Visualization to Support
    Planning." *Ambio* 42.2 (2013): 215-228. Print.
11 Axelsson, Robert, Per Angelstam, Erik Degerman, Sara Teitelbaum, Kjell Andersson,
    Marine Elbakidze, and Marcus K. Drotz. "Social and Cultural Sustainability: Criteria,
    Indicators, Verifier Variables for Measurement and Maps for Visualization to Support
    Planning." *Ambio* 42.2 (2013): 217. Print.
12 "1. Parliamentary Institutions." *Parliament Of Canada*. N.p., n.d. Web. 17 July 2014.
    <http://www.parl.gc.ca/marleaumontpetit/DocumentViewer.aspx?Sec=Ch01&Seq=2&La
    nguage=E>.
13 "Constitution Acts, 1867 to 1982." *Legislative Services Branch*. N.p., n.d. Web. 16 July 2014.
    <http://laws-lois.justice.gc.ca/eng/Const/page-15.html>.
14 "Canadian Human Rights Commission." CHRC. N.p., n.d. Web. 17 July 2014.
    <ttp://www.chrc-ccdp.ca/eng>.
15 Gibbon, John Murray. *Canadian Mosaic: The Making of A Northern Nation*. Toronto: McClelland
    & Stewart, 1938. Print.
16 Leung, H. *Canadian Multiculturalism in the 21st Century: Emerging Challenges and Debates*.
    Canadian Ethnic Studies, 43/44 (3-1), 19-33. 2011
17 Kristof, Nicholas. "It's Now the Canadian Dream." *The New York Times*. The New York Times,
    14 May 2014. Web. 17 July 2014. <http://www.nytimes.com/2014/05/15/opinion/
    kristof-its-now-the-canadian-dream.html?_r=2>.
18 Leonhardt, David, and Kevin Quealy. "The American Middle Class Is No Longer the
    World's Richest." *The New York Times*. The New York Times, 22 Apr. 2014. Web. 17 July 2014.
    <http://www.nytimes.com/2014/04/23/upshot/the-american-middle-class-is-no-longer-
    the-worlds-richest.html>.

19 Adams, Michael. *Fire and Ice: The United States, Canada and the Myth of Converging Values.* Canada: Penguin Group, 2004. 117-118. Print.

20 Berelowitz, Lance. *Dream City: Vancouver and the Global Imagination.* Vancouver, B.C.: Douglas & McIntyre, 2005. 21. Print.

21 Eidse, James. *Vancouver Matters.* Vancouver: Blueimprint, 2008. Print.

22 Metro Vancouver. "2011 Census Bulletin #1 Population and Dwelling Counts." Statistics Canada. <http://www.metrovancouver.org/about/publications/Publications/2011_CensusBulletin1-Pop_and_Dwell.pdf>

23 Berelowitz, Lance. *Dream City: Vancouver and the Global Imagination.* Vancouver, B.C.: Douglas & McIntyre, 2005. 21. Print.

24 Berelowitz, Lance. *Dream City: Vancouver and the Global Imagination.* Vancouver, B.C.: Douglas & McIntyre, 2005. 21. Print.

25 "A Summary of the Livability Ranking and Overview." *The Economist: Intelligence* (2013). Print.

26 "Is Vancouver really Canada's Most Livable City?" *Yahoo News Canada.* N.p., 29 Aug. 2013. Web. 18 July 2014. <https://ca.news.yahoo.com/blogs/pulseofcanada/vancouver-really-canada-most-livable-city-143542459.html>.

27 "A Summary of the Livability Ranking and Overview." *The Economist: Intelligence* (2013). Print.

28 Glaeser, Edward L. *Triumph of the City: How Our Greatest Invention Makes Us Richer, Smarter, Greener, Healthier, and Happier.* New York: Penguin Press, 2011. 239. Print.

29 Metro Vancouver. "2011 National Household Survey – Bulletin #6 Immigration and Cultural Diversity." Statistics Canada. <http://www.metrovancouver.org/about/publications/Publications/2011CensusNo6-immigrationCulturaDiverstiyl.pdf> See also: "NHS Focus on Geography Series – Vancouver." Census Of Canda. Statistics Canada, n.d. Web. 17 July 2014. <http://www12.statcan.gc.ca/nhs-enm/2011/as-sa/fogs-spg/Pages/FOG.cfm?lang=E&level=3&GeoCode=933>.

30 Glaeser, Edward L. *Triumph of the City: How Our Greatest Invention Makes Us Richer, Smarter, Greener, Healthier, and Happier.* New York: Penguin Press, 2011. 240-241. Print.

31 Glaeser, Edward L. *Triumph of the City: How Our Greatest Invention Makes Us Richer, Smarter, Greener, Healthier, and Happier.* New York: Penguin Press, 2011. 239. Print.

32 Lederman, Marsha. "Giving Architects Their Due." *The Globe and Mail.* N.p., 13 Jan. 2010. Web. 29 July 2014. <http://www.theglobeandmail.com/arts/giving-architects-their-due/article1207454/>.

33 Glaeser, Edward L. *Triumph of the City: How Our Greatest Invention Makes Us Richer, Smarter, Greener, Healthier, and Happier.* New York: Penguin Press, 2011. 239-240. Print.

34 Glaeser, Edward L. *Triumph of the City: How Our Greatest Invention Makes Us Richer, Smarter, Greener, Healthier, and Happier.* New York: Penguin Press, 2011. 240. Print.

35 Coupland, Douglas. *City of Glass: Douglas Coupland's Vancouver.* Vancouver, B.C.: Douglas & McIntyre, 2000. Print.

36 Walton, Dawn. "Vancouver Most Expensive City in Canada." *Yahoo Finance Canada.* N.p., 24 July 2013. Web. 17 July 2014. <https://ca.finance.yahoo.com/blogs/insight/vancouver-most-expensive-city-canada-124932291.html>.

37 Glaeser, Edward L. *Triumph of the City: How Our Greatest Invention Makes Us Richer, Smarter, Greener, Healthier, and Happier.* New York: Penguin Press, 2011. 130. Print.

38 Enright, Robert. *Body Heat: The Story of The Woodward's Redevelopment.* Vancouver: Blueimprint, 2010. 333. Print.

39 Enright, Robert. *Body Heat: The Story of The Woodward's Redevelopment.* Vancouver: Blueimprint, 2010. 319-326; 329-333. Print.; Gómez, Alberto. *Towards an Ethical Architecture: Issues Within The Work of Gregory Henriquez.* Vancouver: Blueimprint, 2006. 67-75 Print.

40 Lagueux, Maurice. "Ethics versus Aesthetics in Architecture." *The Philosophical Forum* 35.2 (2004): 117-133. Print.

41 Pérez-Gómez, Alberto. *Towards an Ethical Architecture: Issues Within The Work of Gregory Henriquez.* Vancouver: Blueimprint, 2006. 69. Print.

42 Enright, Robert. *Body Heat: The Story of The Woodward's Redevelopment.* Vancouver: Blueimprint, 2010. 313-314. Print.

43 Chodikoff, Ian. "An Ethical Plan. *Canadian Architect.* 1 Feb. 2007: 38-41. Print.

44 "Greenest City: 2020 Action Plan." *City of Vancouver* (2011): 5. Print.

45 Alini, Erica. "The Most Livable City? "*Maclean's* 19 Sept. 2011: 43. Print.

46 "Median Total Income, by Family Type, by Census Metropolitan Area (All Census Families)." Statistics Canada. Canada.ca, 10 Feb. 2013. Web. 17 July 2014. <http://www.statcan.gc.ca/tables-tableaux/sum-som/l01/cst01/famil107a-eng.htm>.

47 "Metro Vancouver Housing Market Characterized By Modest Home Sale and Price Increases in 2013." *Real Estate Board of Greater Vancouver.* N.p., 3 Jan. 2014. Web. 17 July 2014. <http://www.rebgv.org/news-statistics/metro-vancouver-housing-market-characterized-modest-home-sale-and-price-increases>.

48 Sutherland, Jim. "Extreme Makeover." *Vancouver Magazine* Apr. 2013: 66. Print.

49 Bagli, Charles. "Developers End Fight Blocking 2 More Luxury Towers in Midtown." *The New York Times.* The New York Times, 15 Oct. 2013. Web. 17 July 2014. <http://www.nytimes.com/2013/10/16/nyregion/developers-end-fight-blocking-2-more-luxury-towers-in-midtown.html?pagewanted=all>.

50 Sutherland, Jim. "Extreme Makeover." *Vancouver Magazine* Apr. 2013: 66. Print.

51 "Bold Ideas Towards an Affordable City." *Mayor's Task Force on Housing Affordability* (2012): 4. Print.

52 "Bold Ideas Towards an Affordable City." *Mayor's Task Force on Housing Affordability* (2012): 4. Print.

53 Metro Vancouver. "Metro Vancouver Housing Data Book." Section 3.2. Jan. 2014. Statistics Canada.

54 Hiebert, Daniel, and Kathy Sherrell. "The Integration and Inclusion of Newcomers in British Columbia." *Metropolis British Columbia* 09 - 11 (2009): 10. Print.

55 Hiebert, Daniel, and Kathy Sherrell. "The Integration and Inclusion of Newcomers in British Columbia." *Metropolis British Columbia* 09 - 11 (2009): 12. Print.

56 "Analysis of the Canadian Immigrant Labour Market, 2008 to 2011." *Statistics Canada.* Canada.ca, 19 June 2013. Web. 17 July 2014. <http://www.statcan.gc.ca/pub/71-606-x/2012006/part-partie1-eng.htm>.

57 Hiebert, Daniel. "A New Residential Order?: The Social Geography of Visible Minority and Religious Groups in Montreal, Toronto, and Vancouver in 2031." *Citizenship & Immigration Canada* (2012): 23. Print.

58 NIMBY stands for "Not In My Back Yard."

59 Cotten, M. and Lasprogata, G. "Corporate Citizenship & Creative Collaboration: Best Practices for Cross-Sector Partnerships", *Journal of Law, Business & Ethics*, Volume 18, PG 20 (Winter 2012).

60 Cotten, M. and Lasprogata, G. "Corporate Citizenship & Creative Collaboration: Best Practices for Cross-Sector Partnerships", *Journal of Law, Business & Ethics*, Volume 18, PG 24-25 (Winter 2012). See also: Waddock, S. A.. "Understanding Social Partnerships: An Evolutionary Model of Partnership Organizations."*Administration & Society* 21.1 (1989): 78-100. Print.

61 Cotten, M. and Lasprogata, G. "Corporate Citizenship & Creative Collaboration: Best Practices for Cross-Sector Partnerships", *Journal of Law, Business & Ethics*, Volume 18, PG 25 (Winter 2012).

62 Enright, Robert. *Body Heat: The Story of the Woodward's Redevelopment*. Vancouver: Blueimprint, 2010. 323. Print.

63 Enright, Robert. *Body Heat: The Story of the Woodward's Redevelopment*. Vancouver: Blueimprint, 2010. 324. Print.

64 Punter, John. *The Vancouver Achievement: Urban Planning and Design*. Vancouver: UBC Press, 2003. XV. Print.

65 "Development Permit Board." *City of Vancouver*. N.p., n.d. Web. 20 July 2014. <http://vancouver.ca/home-property-development/development-permit-board.aspx>.

66 "Urban Design Panel." *City of Vancouver*. N.p., n.d. Web. 20 July 2014. <http://vancouver.ca/your-government/urban-design-panel.aspx>.

67 "Development Cost Levies." *City of Vancouver*. N.p., n.d. Web. 20 July 2014. <http://vancouver.ca/home-property-development/development-cost-levies.aspx>.

68 "Community Amenity Contributions." *City of Vancouver*. N.p., n.d. Web. 20 July 2014. <http://vancouver.ca/home-property-development/community-amenity-contributions. aspx>.

69 "Ministry of Community, Sport and Cultural Development." *Community Amenity Contributions: Balancing Community Planning, Public Benefits and Housing Affordability* 1 (2014): 14-16. Print.

70 "Incentives for Developers: Transferable Heritage Density Bonuses." *City of Vacouver*. N.p., n.d. Web. 20 July 2014. <http://vancouver.ca/home-property-development/density-incentives-for-developers.aspx>.

71 "2007 Survey Of Low-Income Housing In The Downtown Core." *Housing Policy Community Services Group* 1 (2007): 1. Print.

72 Linden, Isabelle Aube, Marissa Y. Mar, Gregory R. Werker, Kerry Jang, and Michael Krausz. "Research on a Vulnerable Neighborhood - The Vancouver Downtown Eastside from 2001 to 2011." *Journal of Urban Health: Bulletin of the New York Academy of Medicine* 90.3 (2012) Print.

73 Leidl, P., "Vancouver: prosperity and poverty make uneasy bedfellows in world's most 'liveable' city."UNFPA; 2007.

74 Thompson, Scott. "Policing Vancouver's Mentally Ill: The Disturbing Truth—Beyond Lost in Translation." *Vancouver Police Department* (2010) Print.

75 Linden, Isabelle Aube, Marissa Y. Mar, Gregory R. Werker, Kerry Jang, and Michael Krausz. "Research on a Vulnerable Neighborhood - The Vancouver Downtown Eastside from 2001 to 2011." *Journal of Urban Health: Bulletin of the New York Academy of Medicine* 90.3 (2012) Print.

76 Sinoski, Kelly. "Number of People Sleeping in Vancouver's Streets or on Couches More Than Tripled Since 2011 (updated)." *The Vancouver Sun*. N.p., 23 Apr. 2014. Web. 20 July 2014. <http://www.vancouversun.com/news/Numbe

77 Sinoski, Kelly. "Number of People Sleeping in Vancouver's Streets or on Couches More Than Tripled Since 2011 (updated)." *The Vancouver Sun*. N.p., 23 Apr. 2014. Web. 20 July 2014. <http://www.vancouversun.com/news/Numbe

78 Robertson, G. "Despite Setback, Vancouver's Homeless Plan is On the Right Track." *The Vancouver Sun*. N.p., 28 Apr. 2014. Web. 20 July 2014. <http://www.vancouversun.com/touch/opinion/Despite+setback+Vancouver+homeless+plan+right+track/9785374/story.html?rel=9979290>.

Case Studies
in Vancouver

MARYA COTTEN GOULD

I. Serving the Most Vulnerable

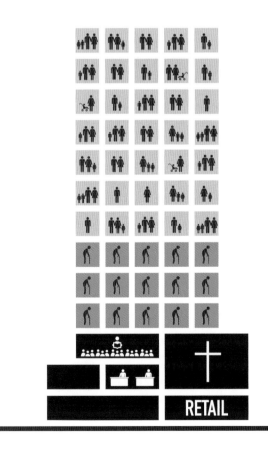

RETAIL

Helping a Church Thrive and Support its Community

Redevelopment of the Central Presbyterian Church

"The ability to leverage the church's free land
in order to build a new sanctuary, daycare,
and non-market seniors' housing that is
all paid for by the market rental housing
is unique to a city like Vancouver."

GREGORY HENRIQUEZ

THE CENTRAL PRESBYTERIAN CHURCH (CPC) is a sanctuary for the worshippers who attend services there, but it also serves as a bustling community hub for Vancouver's West End. It is not a building that is busy on Sundays only. The current building is in almost constant use seven days a week, from six in the morning until 10 at night. To start, there is not just one congregation using the space, there are three. There is the CPC, headed by Reverend Jim Smith (who is known to all simply as Reverend Jim), as well as the Galilee Korean Presbyterian Church. Both are congregations of the Presbyterian Church of Canada. The two are "co-ministries" sharing the same church space and making collaborative decisions, according to Reverend Jim. The third congregation is the Christ Alive Community Church, which ministers to the lesbian, gay, bisexual and transgendered community. Among the three co-ministries, there are about 500 regular congregants.

In addition to the worship services, religious studies, and counselling of the three ministries, the CPC is a hive of community activity at all times. There is a daycare that the CPC has run since the 1970s, the Mole Hill Montessori preschool, after-school care, a summer camp, and youth karate classes. The church hosts free community breakfasts, a

Christmas dinner, and a twice-weekly Bread Ministry with bread donated from the COBS bakery down the street. It is a host site for the Greater Vancouver Food Bank and the location for regular meetings for a 12-step recovery group, ESL classes, and the Out in Harmony Choir. The CPC serves as a location for occasional community meetings held by different groups in the neighbourhood, like the Mole Hill Housing Society, QMUNITY, and the Community Police Association. They regularly host visiting youth and adult church and community groups, and serve as a polling station for elections.

The reality is the current building is dated, the entry dark and unwelcoming, and the existing community and meeting space constrains what the church can do with respect to congregant and community outreach. The church wants to be able to expand their ability to offer midweek worship, Bible studies, and drop-in quiet rooms for prayer and counselling. With more space, the church could also provide more outreach to seniors and activities during the daytime, like lunches, study groups, and health and wellness classes. More meeting space and upgraded kitchens and bathroom facilities (including showers) would facilitate hosting more events, community groups, and visiting groups. The church has visions of being able to do more intercultural and interfaith outreach and dialogue groups, and to accommodate more performing arts like drama, choir, and ensembles.

The need and desire for updated and expanded space was obvious to the CPC, but its leadership was not sure how to go about securing a new sanctuary with better meeting space and facilities. The CPC knew its land was valuable, but they wanted to stay in the neighbourhood and they were not sure how they could fund new construction. As Reverend Jim said, "We've had a dream—a vision—of redeveloping for many years." But how could its leadership afford to redevelop their land?

At a community outreach meeting for the 1401 Comox Project, Gillan Jackson, a trustee of the CPC, was studying the plans for the site of the former St. John's United Church. He mused out loud that the CPC had more land than this site. "Where is this?" someone asked Jackson. That someone was Gregory Henriquez of Henriquez Partners Architects. They ended up chatting briefly about the CPC's land and a desire to secure a new sanctuary, and decided to set up a meeting to discuss the possibility of a new sanctuary in more detail. The CPC then hired Henriquez to evaluate its options. Henriquez created some preliminary pro-forma financial statements and development scenarios, and brought in the BTY Group (BTY) to prepare a formal analysis of the CPC's options. BTY is a quantity surveyor, and serves as a consultant on the costs of construction.

BTY presented the CPC with three possible options. The first option was to sell their valuable land prior to rezoning. The CPC could sell the land to a developer based on the value of the land at its current zoning. The developer would pay to go through the rezoning process and develop the land, including constructing a new church space that the CPC could buy from the developer at cost. The financial models from this scenario showed that the CPC would need to have several million additional dollars to be able to buy the new facility. The second option was that the CPC could rezone the land and sell the rezoned land to a developer and the CPC could receive the new church space as part of

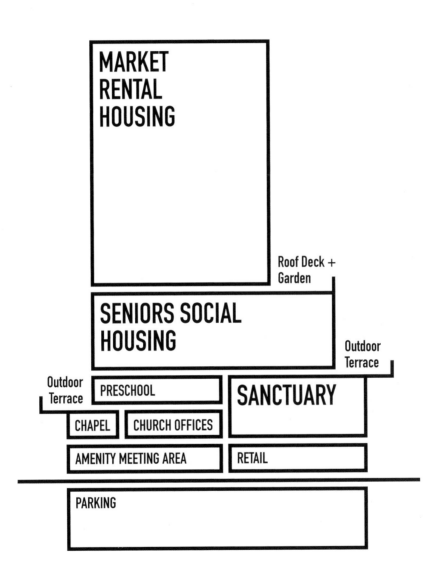

MARKET RENTAL HOUSING

Roof Deck + Garden

SENIORS SOCIAL HOUSING

Outdoor Terrace

Outdoor Terrace

PRESCHOOL

SANCTUARY

CHAPEL

CHURCH OFFICES

AMENITY MEETING AREA

RETAIL

PARKING

PROGRAM DIAGRAM

the deal. The third option was the CPC would act as a developer and redevelop the land itself—it would fund the rezoning, manage the construction, and use the profits from condominium units to construct a new church, and maybe even some housing for seniors as part of the development. The CPC choose the third option, to develop it themselves. Henriquez admitted, "I was shocked. I really thought they'd pursue the second option which is an innovative model in itself, but they wanted to develop it themselves." Reverend Jim noted in a presentation that the CPC congregation decided to pursue the third option, annotating the PowerPoint slide: "We *are* after all, Presbyterian!" (Historically, Presbyterians do not sell their land, according to Reverend Jim.)

The decision to redevelop their site meant the CPC needed a project team and Henriquez believed they needed a construction manager and possibly a project manager as well. Continuing in their role as not just architects but as facilitators for putting together the project and its team, Henriquez Partners made introductions to potential development partners and guided the CPC through the selection process. One of the potential development partners Henriquez Partners introduced to the CPC was Axiom Builders, which is a part of Bosa Properties (Bosa). Bosa is a family-owned development company with a solid reputation, having operated in the Lower Mainland of British Columbia for 50 years. After meeting with several potential development partners, the CPC selected Bosa. The Bosa family is Catholic, not Presbyterian, but as Reverend Jim noted confidently, "They understand church. They've done a lot of work with the Catholic School Board. They understand our needs." Henriquez described the meeting between the CPC and Colin Bosa, the young CEO of Bosa, "Colin, they just loved.... He is a very 'my word is my bond' kind of guy." Bosa promised in collaborating with the CPC that Bosa Properties would take on the risk of development, and that any development plan would include the new church space as well as 42 units of seniors' housing. The CPC had found their development partner.

On June 27, 2012, the CPC, Bosa, and Henriquez Partners held their first community meeting to discuss the possible redevelopment plan before taking any official action with the City of Vancouver. This initial plan called for a tower with a podium on the site, with the new sanctuary space and church facilities located in the podium. Above the church facilities, there would be 42 units of non-market rental housing for seniors, operated by a non-profit housing society that would be established by the CPC. Above the seniors housing would be approximately 90 units of market-rate condominiums. The sale of the condos would help finance the construction of the new church space as well as enable the below-market-rate seniors rentals to be owned by the CPC and operated without needing any government subsidy. The community support at this outreach meeting was strong, even among groups that had been vehemently opposed to the 1401 Comox project, so the team started preliminary discussions with the City of Vancouver about the project proposal.

Then market conditions changed and the condominium market softened. At the same time, the City of Vancouver introduced the new Rental 100 Program, which gives incentives to developers who develop purpose-built rentals. Bosa Properties began to rethink its strategy. What if they could do an all purpose-built rental building and still be able to build the church and the seniors housing in the lower floors? On October 31, 2013, the team filed a combined rezoning and development permit application (the Rental 100 Program enables a concurrent process as part of its expedited process for eligible projects). Furthermore, the West End Community Plan was under development, which generally precluded development in the interim, but the City's policy contained an exception for projects that accommodate the expansion of non-profit, institutional, and cultural uses, and also for projects striving for 30 percent of the units as social or supportive housing. In this case, the CPC redevelopment met both categories of exceptions.

The rezoning and development permit application filed with the City in October 2013 contains a plan for redeveloping the site, in which the CPC will occupy the first three floors of the building. There will be a new sanctuary that seats 300 people, and a smaller chapel that seats 90. There will be office space and more community meeting/event space, as well as a commercial-grade kitchen. On the ground floor, there will be a retail space that will be owned by the CPC and leased most likely to an organization that will provide medical or dental care or other services useful to members of the community. The revenues generated will go to the CPC to support its programs.

Above the church space will be three floors of affordable housing comprising 42 units of non-market housing for seniors and other vulnerable adults. The 42 units will have a range of subsidies. The top 15 floors of the tower will contain 168 market-rate rental apartments, with a mix of studio, one-bedroom, and two-bedroom apartments. The market-rate units will help finance community services and the subsidized housing program. There will be patios for the preschool, the subsidized rental housing, and also the market-rate rental housing.

Henriquez Partners embraced the challenge of designing a building that will have a church with more than one sanctuary, and all of the administrative and programming needs of a religious institution, as well as housing for seniors and vulnerable adults, and a market rental housing tower. First of all, there are construction difficulties in building a residential tower over a large worship space because it requires that the weight of the tower be transferred over the sanctuary. There are also issues of acoustical separation to ensure the necessary level of quiet is achieved in the sanctuary. This kind of building can only be economically feasible to build—especially with the added cost of transferring the load of the building—because land values are so high in Vancouver and the CPC had no land acquisition costs.

Another important design consideration is to develop a religious sanctuary and worship space that still has a spiritual essence when it is also part of a modern residential tower. As Reverend Jim described it, there must be a "pilgrimage to the place of worship". Henriquez Partners took several steps to try to capture the spirituality of the space in their design and to demarcate the space as a place of worship. The stained glass cross from the current sanctuary will be preserved and used in the new sanctuary as a symbol of continuity and identity. Henriquez Partners selected fritted glass for the portions of the building associated with the CPC in order to create a reflective, translucent building exterior for the podium, which will set it apart from the rest of the tower, and be particularly luminous when lit at night.

The sanctuary's interior wood finish will be visible from the street which will help accentuate the idea of the pilgrimage to the site of worship. The wood is a conscious part of the design. The church leadership, always cognizant of the diversity of the congregants, wanted the sanctuary to be immediately identifiable as a Presbyterian space, but also have an inclusive design that would appeal to many cultures, including Asian and First Nations communities. This emphasis on inclusivity dates back to 15 years ago when the CPC was struggling and in debt. The church leadership at the time decided according to Reverend Jim to "not only survive but thrive by understanding that the congregation needs to be relevant to the community where it finds itself." The primary goal of the new sanctuary design is for anyone entering it to think, "This is a place where I can meet God."

During construction of the new sanctuary, the CPC will need temporary space to inhabit for up to two years, and all of the groups that use its space currently will move too. "Everyone is coming," declares Reverend Jim, symbolizing the inclusive nature of his ministry and the far-reaching community the church serves beyond its congregants. On October 25, 2015, the CPC held their final service prior to the demolition of the existing sanctuary. The new sanctuary and the rental units are expected to be open in the fall of 2017. Every development project has its hiccups, but Reverend Jim remains calm and assured that everything will work out in the end. "This is, after all," he says, "a God-driven project."

A non-profit housing society will be formed by the CPC to operate the 42 units of non-market housing for seniors and other vulnerable adults. The targeted rental subsidies for the 42 units are: 40 percent of the units with a "deep subsidy" (50 percent below market rates), 40 percent of the units with a "shallow subsidy" (80 percent of market rates), and the remaining 20 percent of units slightly below market (90 percent of market rates).

History of Central Presbyterian Church

The Presbyterians have a long history in Vancouver, dating back to 1886 when the First Presbyterian Church was built (which is also the year that Vancouver was incorporated). It was later destroyed by a fire and subsequently rebuilt. A second Presbyterian Church, St. Andrew's, was built at Georgia and Richards streets in 1888. A third Presbyterian Church was added in 1902 when St. John's was built at the corner of Comox and Broughton. In 1925, St. John's voted to join the Methodist and Congregational churches of the newly formed United Church of Canada. (St. John's United Church sold its land to developers for the 1401 Comox project described in Part II of the Case Studies.)

The "Continuing Presbyterians" from St. John's joined with congregants from St. Andrew's and they formed the CPC. They then purchased a Congregationalist building at 1100 Thurlow at the northeast corner of Thurlow and Pendrell Streets. A land-swap deal in 1975 with St. Paul's Hospital for their needed expansion meant a new CPC facility was built across the street from its original site. 1155 Thurlow has been the home for CPC for over 35 years. Since 1998, the Galilee Korean Presbyterian Church and the Christ Alive Community Church have also called this church their own. The new sanctuary will be built on this site.

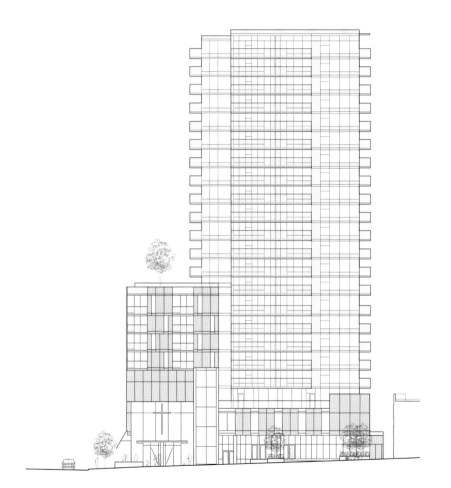

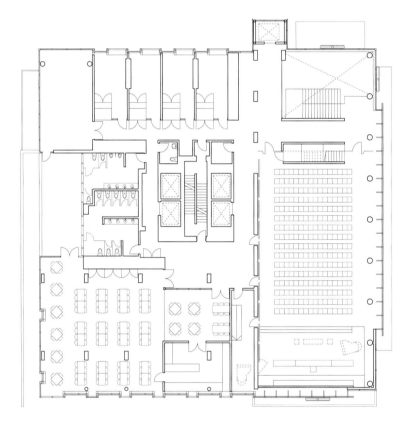

CPC SECOND FLOOR PLAN

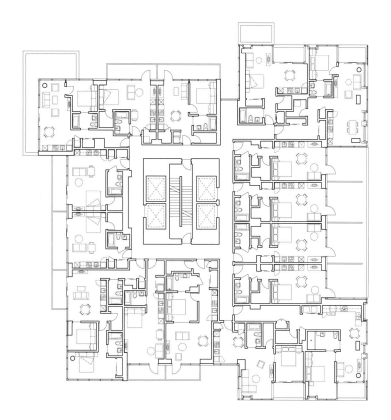

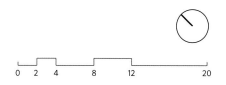

0   2   4   8   12   20

CPC TYPICAL RESIDENTIAL
FLOOR PLAN

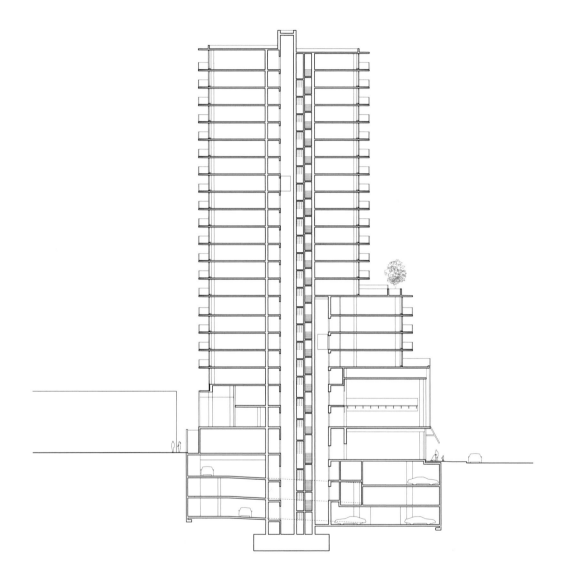

CPC SECTION

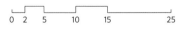

0 2 5   10   15   25

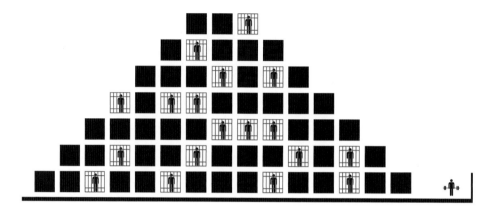

A Poetic Transformation from Jail to Social Housing
250 Powell

"The poetic metaphor of transforming a jail into housing is the healthiest message any society can send to its next generation."

GREGORY HENRIQUEZ

IN VANCOUVER'S Downtown Eastside, a building at 211 Gore Street underwent a dramatic and positive metamorphosis, from an empty jail to affordable housing. Heavy security elements were stripped from the building, and former jail cells were demolished. In the building's shell, 96 units of social and affordable housing were constructed, 38 of which are designated for exclusive rental to participants of the BladeRunners program, a non-profit work training program for at-risk Aboriginal youth. The detainees' former gymnasium became a shared amenity space with a kitchen for the new residents and surrounding community. The exercise yard for the previous detainees was redesigned into a community garden with flowers and vegetables. From start to finish, this poetic transformation of a jail into housing is a Henriquez story.

In the late 1970s, the provincial government of British Columbia hired Richard Henriquez, Gregory's father and founder of Henriquez Partners Architects, to design a new remand centre that would hold individuals charged with crimes and considered unfit for release on bail while their cases were being adjudicated. The accused would need to be brought in front of a judge to check on their well-being at regular intervals. Due to this requirement, remand centres were built all over

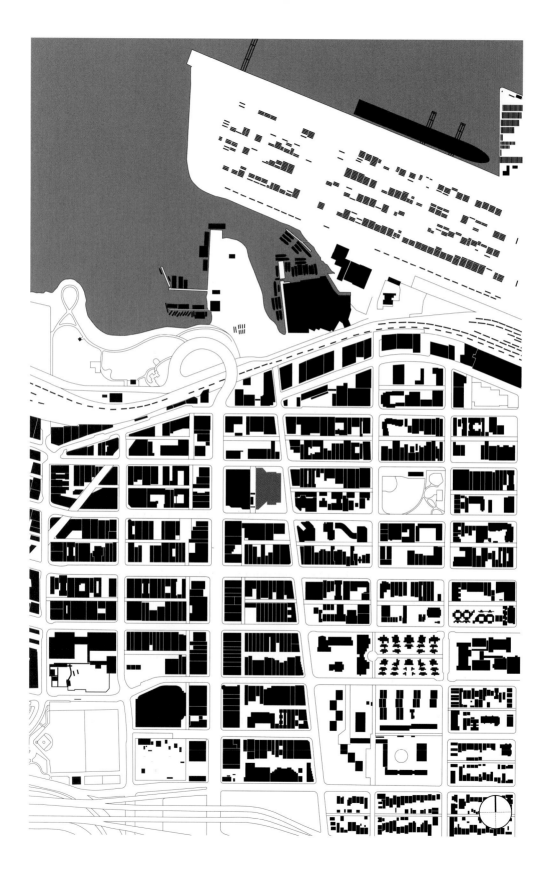

North America, usually located in downtown cores, conveniently placed near police stations and court buildings. Completed by Richard Henriquez in 1981, the building was designed to be secure as a remand centre and had tunnels which connected it to the Provincial Court of British Columbia and the Vancouver Police Department. The Vancouver Pretrial Services Centre officially opened for use in 1983.

In addition to the obvious security concerns, Richard Henriquez designed the Gore Street building with a clear respect for the principle that individuals are innocent until proven guilty. There was an exercise yard, a gymnasium, and outdoor decks on each floor, which, in spite of the required security measures, provided the detainees with fresh air and views. The façade of the building had concrete pods that jutted out, which served as the sleeping alcoves for the prisoners. It was a visible metaphor of the "half in jail, half in society" state of the people currently imprisoned, yet still presumed innocent, and not yet tried or convicted.

With the advent of video conferencing and webcams, the proximity of the remand centre to the courthouse became less crucial and, across North America, remand centres were increasingly sited outside of downtown cores. The Vancouver Pretrial Services Centre closed in 2002. The last detainees held there were suspected of being the terrorists responsible for the 1985 bombing of Air India Flight 182.

Since the remand centre closed in 2002, it has been vacant, except to house Vancouver's Downtown Community Court, which opened in its basement and ground floor in September 2008 as a pilot project by the Provincial Court of British Columbia, the Ministry of the Attorney General and other government and community partners. It is Canada's first community court, based partly on an innovative model emerging from the Brooklyn, New York neighbourhood of Red Hook. The model focusses on trying to address the causes of neighbourhood crime, such as addiction and mental illness, by providing offenders with referrals to services in order to prevent repeat offenses and having offenders provide reparations to the community with community-based service. The Downtown Community Court continues to operate out of the building on its ground floor (with an address of 211 Gore Street) and is separate from the new residential component of the building (with a new address of 250 Powell Street).

In 2008, as the sluggish Canadian economy meant few new projects for architects (including Henriquez Partners) Gregory Henriquez decided to put the firm's idle architects to work on an idea for a housing project he had been contemplating. Could he redesign his father's now empty remand centre into much-needed housing in the Downtown Eastside of Vancouver? Would government officials agree that it was an inspired and sensible idea?

With a plan in hand, Gregory Henriquez approached Craig Crawford, then vice president of development at BC Housing, about the idea of renovating the empty remand centre to turn it into rental housing. The idea was an appealing one for BC Housing—the process of renovating an existing empty building can be more economical and quicker than building from the ground up. The initial idea was for self-financing rentals that would not require government subsidy, however, the community and the City of Vancouver pushed for a mix of housing that would be more inclusive. Such a housing mix would support the City's and the Provincial Government's goals of more housing for the region

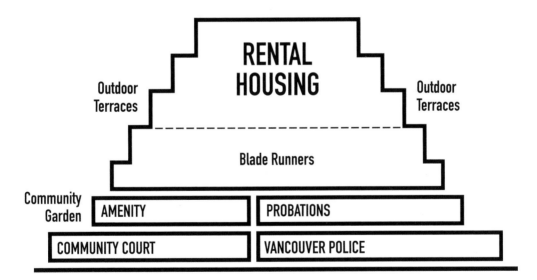

RENTAL
HOUSING

Outdoor
Terraces

Outdoor
Terraces

Blade Runners

Community
Garden

AMENITY

PROBATIONS

COMMUNITY COURT

VANCOUVER POLICE

PROGRAM DIAGRAM

(especially social and affordable rental housing) however, it also meant that government funding would be necessary in order to go forward with the project.

In May 2011, City Council approved a grant of $2 million: $1 million to be paid when the building permit was issued, and the remaining $1 million when the occupancy permit was issued. The remaining funding would be provided by BC Housing and through a commercial mortgage. The City and BC Housing debated the proper mix of housing. One critical issue was whether any ongoing subsidy for the operation would be required from BC Housing if the units did not contain an affordable market rental component. The City wanted to prioritize having units that were rented at the shelter rate of housing. The City also had guidelines and policies about the layout and size of the units that would need to be considered in the design process. Additionally, there were concerns about having people living in the building with the security complications of having the Downtown Community Court in the building as well as a police station and other courts nearby.

However, with patience, the plan took shape for six floors of housing, which includes 14 one-bedroom suites (ranging in size from 411 to 560 square feet) and 82 studio suites (from 316 to 456 square feet). Two floors of housing will provide 38 suites for participants of the Blade-Runners program. Twenty-four units will be rented at the shelter rate of government income assistance, currently $375/month. The balance of the units will be rented at rates at or below what is considered "affordable" by the Canada Mortgage and Housing Corporation Housing Income Limit. In 2011, these levels were a salary of $32,500 for a studio and $36,300 for a one bedroom.

A plan in place, BC Housing, in consultation with the City of Vancouver, selected the Bloom Group (originally founded in 1961 as the

St. James Community Service Society) to be the developer, manager, and ongoing operator of 250 Powell. The Bloom Group has operated as a housing, health, and social services provider in the Downtown Eastside of Vancouver for more than 50 years. They run several shelters for women and children, and operate buildings that provide mental health housing, supportive housing, and affordable housing. They also administer a hospice care program and an adult guardianship program for the elderly and other vulnerable adults. As the manager and operator of 250 Powell, the Bloom Group will serve as the landlord for all of the units, including the units for participants of the BladeRunners program.

BladeRunners was created as a pilot project in 1994 when General Motors Place (now Rogers Arena) was being constructed. Downtown Eastside activist Jim Green championed the concept by successfully getting 25 at-risk youth from the neighbourhood hired for construction jobs on the arena. The BladeRunners program, now led in Vancouver by Garry Jobin, is a job-training program for youth (generally aged 15-30, depending on the region) that often leads to employment in the construction industry. Approximately 95 percent of the youth in their program are Aboriginal, and over 80 percent are homeless or disguised homeless.

Program participants face multiple barriers to employment including a lack of education, a history of being in foster care or lacking familial support, homelessness, a history of physical abuse or drug use, and a criminal history. At the same time, many of them have survived with very little support from anyone and have proven successful with some encouragement and support. By 1996, the Province of British Columbia had given formal support for the program and it quickly spread from Vancouver to other regions of the province as well. After several attempts over time to procure designated housing for the

BladeRunners participants, Green successfully lobbied BC Housing for the inclusion of the BladeRunners as tenants in the 250 Powell project. In 2014, the BladeRunners program celebrated its 20 year anniversary.

The program participants receive safety and carpentry training, as well as some cultural training to help them feel reconnected to their communities and build their esteem. The BladeRunners coordinators also meet participants on the construction site on their first day to provide support, and all along encourage communication and diligent follow-up so that the participants learn to communicate with their employers and co-workers. The program also provides other around-the-clock support, knowing that the BladeRunners will not be able to succeed in their newly found employment if they are not in a stable place in their lives. Thus the program provides support services like finding housing, learning how to budget, accessing community and cultural resources like addiction support programs, athletic leagues, drumming circles, and counselling. Pigeon Park Savings, a partnership between Vancity and PHS Community Services Society, provides banking services for the BladeRunners participants.

The participants have a three-month performance review with the contractor employing them. If all goes well, it can be the path to an apprenticeship, or a way back to school with new confidence in their skills. According to the BladeRunners program, after two years, 80 percent of the participants are still employed in the construction industry and are no longer receiving income assistance (with 30 per-cent of those eventually going on to achieve journeymen status or becoming entrepreneurs). For the BladeRunners, the tangible results of their construction work are reflected in the city skyline, which they can proudly point out as the results of their work to their families. Even if some of the participants chose to follow another employment path, they leave the program with job experience, references, often in a more stable position with regards to housing. There are, of course, challenges and setbacks for some of the BladeRunners, but often the participants return again, motivated to succeed this time, and having a better foundation through training, job contacts, and knowledge of other resources.

Even for the BladeRunner participants who succeed quickly, there are challenges—the pressure that comes from an extended family or community who want assistance from the BladeRunner who has "made it." Jobin, who has worked for the program for the last 18 years, asserts, "We absolutely have to teach them—don't get too low when things go badly and don't get too high when things go great." But, as Jobin says, every time there is a BladeRunner who has achieved the stability of steady employment, housing, and being able to provide for himself or herself and any family members, the program speaks for itself. "The BladeRunners themselves are the best ambassadors for this program," he says.

A tremendous amount of the program involves relationship building with developers, contractors, trade unions, and the construction workers on site. The construction industry has developed a certain amount of belief and trust in the program over time, asserts Jobin, so that, "even when one participant doesn't work out on site, the contractor won't withdraw from the program, but will call and say, 'This BladeRunner isn't ready. But please, send us another kid.'"

Henriquez Partners has worked with the BladeRunners program since the very beginning on many of their projects. For example, Bruce Ericksen Place and the Lore Krill Housing Co-op. For the Woodward's Redevelopment, Jim Green and Henriquez Partners encouraged the

developer Westbank to use BladeRunners on the project. Westbank's president, Ian Gillespie, became such a supporter of the program that he has now committed to use some BladeRunner participants on all of his projects (even including some out-of-province projects like a luxury hotel development in Toronto).

BladeRunners has experience with BC Housing too. Some Blade-Runners live in housing owned or operated by BC Housing, and other BladeRunners have worked on constructing housing projects for the agency. As for the Bloom Group, Jobin said he had never personally worked with the non-profit prior to this project, but complimented executive director Jonathan Oldman and his staff by saying that they have been "nothing but first class to work with."

The vision of quickly renovating the existing remand centre did not materialize, as the project faltered at times due to BC Housing's funding issues, even as all the partners worked to bring the project to fruition. Gregory Henriquez admitted wryly, "This is a great example of the reality that even a project that everyone agrees is a really good idea and where the partners work well together . . . it can still take a really long time."

In some ways, this project is a story decades in the making. Blade-Runners has been striving for 20 years to fulfill Jim Green's vision that BladeRunners should have designated housing to support its participants. He knew that housing, like the life skills support and mentoring, was critical to stabilize the participants so that the job-training program could work. Just a few days before his death in 2012, Green told a reporter for *The Tyee* about the 250 Powell project and the evolution of the BladeRunners program. "Finally after all these years, we have brought these elements together so they have a place with mentors, elders, all they need to make this a really functioning society within a larger society," he said.

This project contains the continuity of history in many other ways. The design mantle has been passed from father to son for the same building for very different uses, but with both architects deeply concerned about granting dignity to the individuals who have inhabited and will inhabit the building. Gregory Henriquez took the time and initiative to come up with a plan to convert the empty remand centre into housing, which he has described as a "poetic metaphor" that is the "healthiest message any society can send to its next generation." The province and City recognized an opportunity to work together to add much-needed social and affordable rentals in the Downtown Eastside, and hired the Bloom Group to operate this project in the neighbourhood where they have served the most vulnerable with unflagging commitment for half a century. Due to the perseverance of the project team over eight years, the housing was completed in the summer of 2015, finally fulfilling Jim Green's decades-long dream of having dedicated housing for the BladeRunners program.

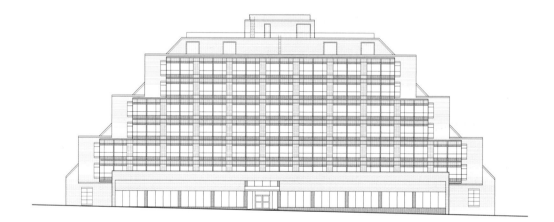

250 POWELL
ELEVATION EAST

0 2   5   10   15   25

0   5   10   20   35

250 POWELL
FLOOR PLAN LEVEL 4

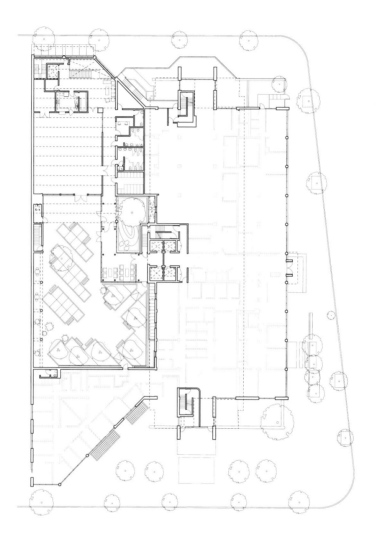

250 POWELL
GROUND FLOOR PLAN

0   5   10   20   35

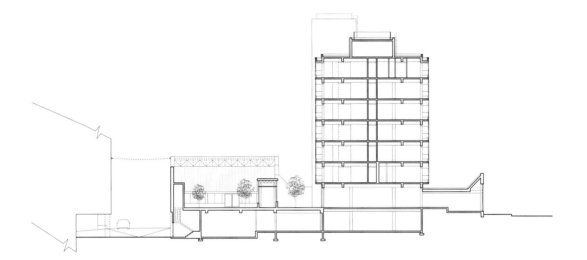

0 2 5   10   15   25

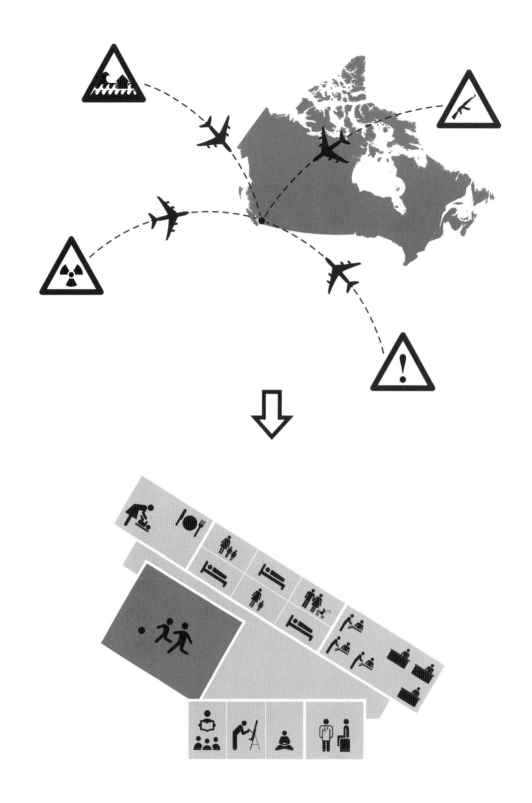

A First of its Kind: Integrated Refugee Services Hub

Immigrant Services Society of British Columbia's Welcome House Centre

"Everyone has the right to seek and to enjoy in other countries asylum from persecution."

ARTICLE 14 OF THE UNITED NATIONS'
UNIVERSAL DECLARATION OF HUMAN RIGHTS

THE AVERAGE CANADIAN sees news stories about war and genocide but thankfully has no idea what it is like to be a refugee: to be forced to flee your country, culture and home, never to return, because you fear for the lives of yourself and your family. That profound fear makes leaving everything familiar seem like the best solution even if you will arrive somewhere foreign, unable to communicate, and possessing only the clothes you are wearing. Refugees are victims of persecution based on race, ethnic identity, political or cultural affiliation, gender, sexual orientation, or religion. Unlike immigrants, refugees do not leave their country of origin by choice, nor is there an option to return. Many refugees who find their way to Canada have been the victims of famine, rape, torture, and violence. They are shell-shocked and wounded mentally and often physically. As a result, it is critical that when refugees arrive in a new country they have support and a sense of safety.

The new Welcome House Centre being developed by the Immigrant Services Society of British Columbia (ISSBC) is essential to their mission of providing newly arrived refugees to British Columbia with a safe haven and the support services needed to begin a new life

← **ISSBC**
Located at 2610 Victoria Drive, close
to the Commercial-Broadway Sky-
Train station with access to the
Millenium Line, the Expo Line, and
several major bus routes.

in Canada. ISSBC provides extensive settlement, language and employment services to immigrants as well as refugees in British Columbia. ISSBC's vision for the Welcome House Centre is to become an innovative hub for the region, providing integrated support services for the refugee community in one location, including co-locating government outreach offices and other non-profit organizations serving the same clients. Co-location helps mitigate the cost and difficulty for traumatized refugees of going to different locations for support services, a process that if too onerous may cause refugees to miss out on receiving much-needed services like healthcare, counseling, legal help, language support, and food banks.

ISSBC has been working with the refugee community in British Columbia for many years. A group of volunteers started the organization in 1968, before incorporating in 1972, to handle the arrival of Ismaili refugees fleeing Idi Amin in Uganda. Today, they have a staff of over 350 and over 800 active volunteers. In an average year, they serve 23,000 immigrant and refugee clients. While ISSBC serves immigrants from around the world and refugees from any program with their settlement, language, and employment services, the new Welcome House Centre will focus primarily on helping government-assisted refugees from the time they first arrive in Canada.

ISSBC has a current Welcome House Centre for government-sponsored refugees located at 530 Drake Street in the Yaletown neighbourhood of Vancouver. The current 70-bed facility has been serving recently arrived refugees for four decades, but the space is cramped and does not offer a lot of flexibility. The now-fashionable Yaletown location is also a difficult one for refugees trying to feed their families on a modest governmental assistance stipend with groceries purchased from the neighbourhood's upscale grocery stores. ISSBC has been dreaming for a long time of a larger Welcome House, with more beds and a greater ability to provide integrated support services on site.

A larger Welcome House would allow for more refugee first-stage housing (for the first few weeks of their arrival in Canada) as well as second-stage housing (up to a year) for those needing extra support. On the ISSBC's wish list for the new space was flexible housing units that can be altered to fit the needs of clients with a variety of family sizes. They also desired a building that was not only large and functional, but would also make the refugees feel safe and create a sense of community.

Sustaining ISSBC's vision for a new Welcome House Centre and turning it into a reality has been a major exercise in perseverance. "I know we've been working on it for at least as long as I've been around . . . the last 15 years for sure," says ISSBC CEO Patricia Woroch. According to Woroch, the new planned Welcome House Centre is the third concerted attempt during her tenure to obtain a new facility. Over a decade ago, a developer offered them new space in one of its developments but the ISSBC Board of Directors perceived the risk as too great and turned down the opportunity. In a second attempt, ISSBC hired people to find land for a new site. They had rounds of discussions with the City of Vancouver and BC Housing about a new location, but nothing materialized. As the Yaletown area became more desirable, developers would

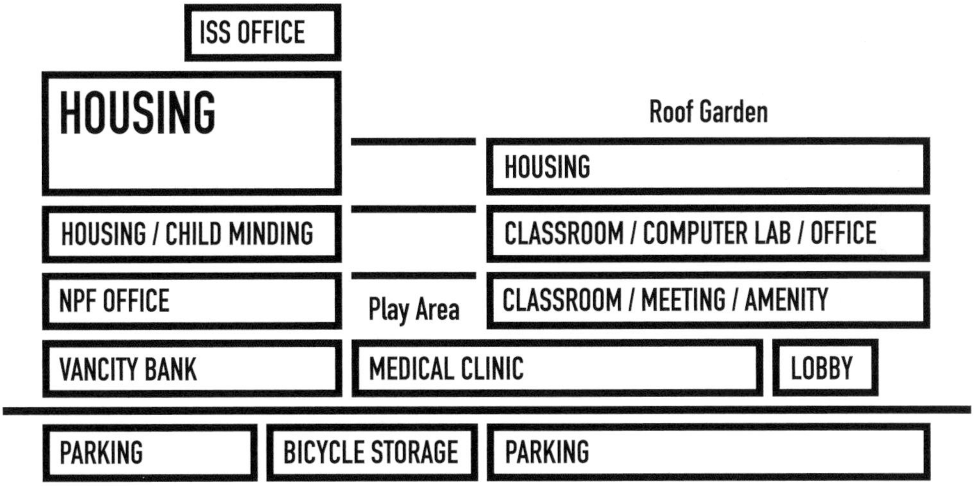

ISS OFFICE

HOUSING

Roof Garden

HOUSING

HOUSING / CHILD MINDING

CLASSROOM / COMPUTER LAB / OFFICE

NPF OFFICE

Play Area

CLASSROOM / MEETING / AMENITY

VANCITY BANK

MEDICAL CLINIC

LOBBY

PARKING

BICYCLE STORAGE

PARKING

PROGRAM DIAGRAM

intermittently offer to purchase the ISSBC location and relocate ISSBC elsewhere. These negotiations never really progressed past the initial stage, and the replacement site offered was often too small. ISSBC even considered relocating a new Welcome House Centre outside of Vancouver, due to the perceived inability to get government funding and the cost of real estate in the city. ISSBC grappled with over a decade of fits and starts of interest, political will, and promises of funding that ultimately went nowhere.

The third substantial attempt had more promising hallmarks as a dedicated team from the non-profit, city government, and private sector emerged. The ISSBC staff and Board of Directors are committed to the undertaking and the success of the new Welcome House Centre. Vickie Jo Morris, a senior social planner in the Social Development Department of the City of Vancouver became a champion of the project. In her discussions with ISSBC about the idea of a new Welcome House Centre, she suggested that ISSBC do a new programmatic study in order to get the project moving forward. She suggested Gregory Henriquez at Henriquez Partners Architects as someone who might be able to help formulate the organization's ideal program and develop a conceptual design that would assist ISSBC in getting the necessary partners on board. (Morris and Henriquez have worked together on several projects in the past that had community programming elements. The first project that they worked on together was Bruce Eriksen Place, a social housing project that was completed in 1997.)

In their initial meetings, Henriquez impressed Woroch with his infectious enthusiasm and Henriquez Partners was engaged to do the programmatic study and conceptual design. ISSBC wanted architects who understood their programming needs as well as understanding that inanimate objects like buildings should be socially transformative, not just functional. That criteria led to ISSBC selecting Henriquez Partners as the architecture firm to design the proposed building, lead any rezoning efforts, and manage the development permitting process. As Woroch described the Henriquez Partners team, "They got that it's more than bricks and mortar, and that's a really big thing . . . . Understanding you can create a community within a building. It is movement and flow that creates community."

ISSBC and Henriquez Partners worked closely with the staff in various departments at the City of Vancouver—Real Estate Services, Business Planning and Services, Social Infrastructure, Social Development, Community Services Group, and Social Policy—to identify a suitable City-owned site. The City staffers also worked hard to locate funding within the City's budget to be able to grant ISSBC a 60-year ground lease for only $1.00. (As a City-owned site, their real estate endowment fund must receive the fair market value for use of the site.) The value of the lease, according to City staff, is the equivalent of $2.7 million. Henriquez, Michael Flanigan (then the City's director of real estate services), and Chris Friesen (ISSBC's director of settlement services) spent time evaluating possible sites for the new Welcome House Centre. Henriquez recalled that when the three of them drove over and saw the 2610 Victoria Drive location on the Eastside of Vancouver, there was immediately a recognition by all three that without a question, "This was the site where we could make this happen."

In April 2013, Vancouver City Council authorized the transaction for the ground lease and up to $490,000 in a capital grant based on $5,000 per lockable room as part of the City's Supportive Housing Strategy and Housing and Homelessness Strategy. At the time, the site was being used as part of the Mayor's Homeless Emergency Action Team (HEAT) and Winter Response low-barrier shelter initiative as

longer-term solutions were identified. The site is ideal for supportive housing because it is conveniently located near public transit, including access to two SkyTrain lines, several major bus routes, retail, and services. The housing it will provide for refugees is a critical component in helping prevent homelessness among a particularly vulnerable population who arrive in Canada without a safety net and who could easily become homeless.

From the Provincial Government, there was not the level of support that ISSBC had hoped would materialize. Over the years, there had been a variety of levels of support and involvement discussed with BC Housing. Several years ago, at the beginning of the effort, ISSBC received a lump sum from BC Housing as seed money. BC Housing's current commitment is the dedication of $500,000 in project development funds to assist in the rezoning and development permit phase of the new Welcome House Centre.

Since ISSBC is a non-profit that lacks experience developing real estate, they needed help to get the new Welcome House Centre built and selected Terra Housing Consultants (Terra Housing) to provide this service through a Request for Proposals. Terra Housing plays the crucial role of managing the development process and the necessary contractors and consultants on behalf of ISSBC. Woroch laughingly described Terra Housing's role as a kind of "translator" for her during the construction process. She says Henriquez Partners and Terra Housing have gone beyond their traditional roles and served as staunch advocates as well as informal political facilitators and fundraisers. Henriquez Partners and Terra Housing have teamed up for more than two decades on successful socially-conscious developments, including the affordable housing projects Bruce Eriksen Place and Lore Krill Housing Co-op, and the groundbreaking Woodward's Redevelopment.

The transitional housing in the Welcome House Centre will have lockable, flexible unit configurations that will allow ISSBC to house singles as well as families with up to 16 members. The current design provides for 18 units of housing that can have the flexibility to provide up to 166 beds. In addition to housing and classroom space, the building will contain offices and clinical space to allow for an efficient concentration of support services for refugees. This ease of access from having co-located services is essential for people who can fail to receive the services they need if they have to visit multiple locations. As Woroch explained, "A lot of the clients that we see, particularly the refugees, are pretty traumatized, so we need to do whatever we can do to make it as painless and as easy as possible for them. They're often times so traumatized that it's even hard to make very simple decisions and sometimes just having to go across town [for services] can be huge."

The Welcome House Centre will serve as a regional primary health clinic, a legal clinic, and a food bank. There will also be trauma and language support. The Department of Citizenship and Immigration of Canada, the Ministry of Social Development Canada, and Service Canada will have government outreach offices located there. Other non-profits serving refugees will also be located within the Welcome House to increase service coordination and efficiency—The Inland Refugee Society, Settlement Orientation Services, Vancouver Association of Survivors of Torture, and Mount Pleasant Family Centre's Circle of Care and Connection Early Childhood Development Refugee Program. Vancity is discussing providing an onsite banking kiosk and ATM machine for the benefit of both clients and staff, and has been incredibly generous in helping to fund the project.

In addition to being functionally appropriate for the programming of ISSBC and other refugee-serving non-profits, the building will also be aesthetically suited to its purpose. It is designed to be a welcoming and pleasing space, filled with light. It will be green—the site will be extensively landscaped and constructed to meet the standards equivalent to a LEED gold certification. The building will also have an expansive entry way and several communal, family oriented-spaces with a child-minding space (including an outdoor playground), a family space, and youth drop in space.

The Welcome House Centre will become a community within itself, as well as being part of the larger Kensington Cedar Cottage neighbourhood where it is situated. The community was very supportive of the project during the rezoning process. Pastor Trevor Vanderveen of the First Christian Reformed Church, the soon to be next-door neighbours of the Welcome House Centre, came out in staunch support of the project, noting that some members of his congregation are ethnic Europeans who came to Canada for refuge after World War II, and may feel a natural affinity to the newly arrived refugees.

As the Welcome House Centre construction nears completion, news headlines regarding the ongoing Syrian refugee crisis highlight the urgency and importance of ISSBC's work. In November 2015, the Government of Canada announced it would welcome 25,000 Syrian refugees before the end of February 2016. The need for asylum worldwide is unabated and Canada will need to continue providing leadership in responding to the humanitarian crises around the world. In bringing in the new refugees, in addition to immigrants, Canada will also face the challenge of nation-building—how to give the diverse newcomers the support needed to make their new lives and thrive in Canada and to feel included in the vibrant, prosperous multi-cultural society that generates so much pride for Canadians. ISSBC will continue to play a critical role for the province and the nation in supporting and helping to incorporate some of the most vulnerable members of Canadian society.

So why will this third attempt to build the new Welcome House Centre succeed when prior attempts did not? "Hearts are all in the right place on the team," concludes Patricia Woroch. ISSBC had a passionate vision of this Welcome House Centre, which was turned into a beautiful and workable building designed by Henriquez Partners that is being constructed with Terra Housing's facilitation on land owned by an enlightened city. Gregory Henriquez describes his firm's design aspirations in the same heart-centered terms, "Our goal was to create a real sense of community and safety while trying to create a heart for it." The new Welcome House Centre will be filled with devoted non-profits and government outreach offices providing services and creating a community the refugees so desperately need.

In the fulfillment of ISSBC's long-awaited dream for a new Welcome House Centre, the project is now 100 percent funded and the official groundbreaking took place on June 20, 2014, to correspond with World Refugee Day. The current schedule has the new Welcome House Centre opening its doors in the spring 2016, with an official grand opening celebration on World Refugee Day 2016.

Refugees in Canada

Canadians are proud of their compassionate desire for humanitarian action and have a long history of embracing refugees, including thousands of enslaved Africans (and their American descendants born into slavery) fleeing the United States through the Underground Railroad in the 19th century. In the latter part of the 20th century, the list of refugees finding a home in Canada reads as a history lesson about violent conflict and genocide around the world: Eastern Europeans displaced by Soviet invasion and National Socialism (Nazism) in the 1940s and 1950s, Chinese fleeing the violence of the Cultural Revolution in the 1960s, Vietnamese "boat people" and Khmer Cambodians fleeing their countries in the 1970s and 1980s with the violent aftermath of the communist victories; and the Kosovars in the 1990s fleeing widespread genocide in the Balkans. In 2012, Canada welcomed 5,412 government-sponsored refugees, of which 711 were received in British Columbia, primarily from Afghanistan, Iran, Somalia, Iraq, and Bhutan. The 2012 level of government-sponsored refugees was the lowest number Canada has had since the 1970s, which concerns many refugee advocates about the direction of federal policy and funding. These advocates question whether Canada is doing enough at a humanitarian level: both in the number of refugees admitted and sponsored, and the level of support once in Canada.

The Canadian refugee system is comprised of two main programs: the In-Canada Asylum Program is for people making claims for refugee status and protection from within Canada, and the Refugee and Humanitarian Resettlement Program allows individuals designated by the United Nations High Commissioner for Refugees and other referral organizations to enter Canada for protection. Refugees can be privately sponsored by ethnic, religious, or community groups who guarantee their financial support, or are sponsored by the Canadian government which provides funding for basic food and shelter for the first year.

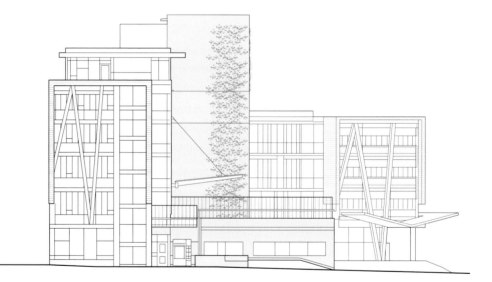

ISSBC
WEST ELEVATION

0   2   4   8   12   20

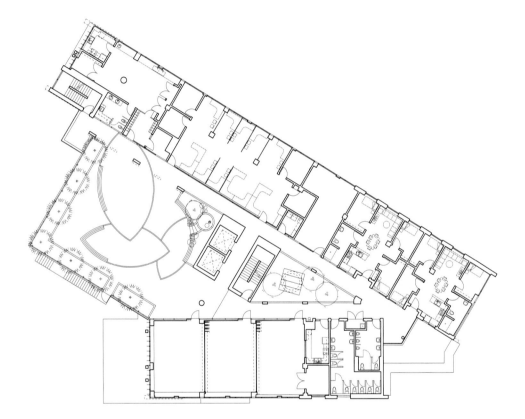

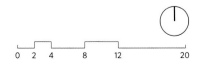

0 2 4   8   12   20

ISSBC
FLOOR PLAN LEVEL 2

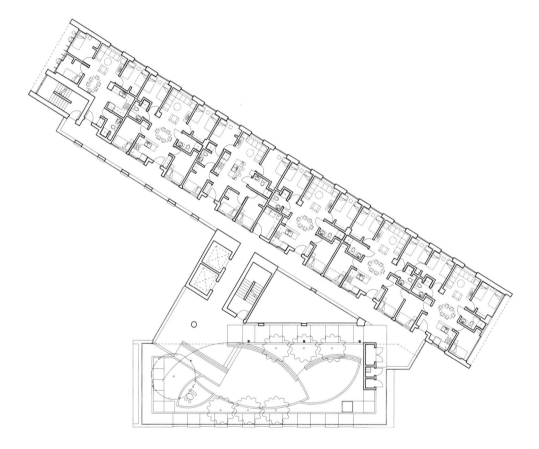

ISSBC
FLOOR PLAN LEVEL 5

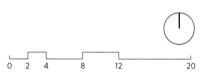

0   2   4   8   12   20

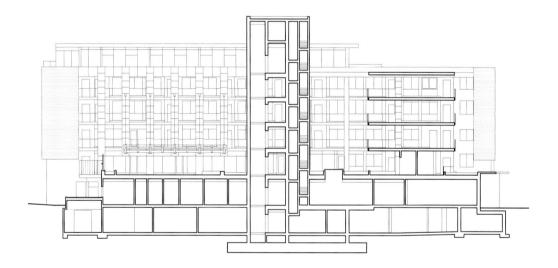

0 2 4   8   12   20

II. Promoting Culture & Creating Community

EXTERIOR

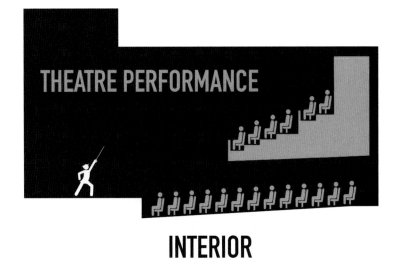

INTERIOR

Saving a Cherished 100-Year-Old Community Theatre
York Theatre Revitalization

"I think that it was just one of those really unique times when everything fell into place. I've always said about this project and just about any other project I've worked on: as long as you find people who can say yes, you're good."

HEATHER REDFERN

THE REDUCTION OF public gathering and performance space in Vancouver, as well as the difficulty in supporting a vibrant cultural scene in the city, has garnered attention recently. Part of the cause is something facing arts organizations all over North America—the changing way that entertainment is consumed. An example is that cinemas are struggling as people are more likely to watch movies at home or on personal devices. The public arena has increasingly been replaced by small electronics and earbuds.

Vancouver also has unique challenges to its arts scene. Its residents are often more focussed on outdoor recreation in the area's many natural assets rather than its cultivated ones. There are very few corporate headquarters located in Vancouver that can fund the arts, yet corporate sponsorship has increasingly become an important basis for supporting the arts as government funding has been reduced. In North America, and most prominently in Canada, the model of the past, where the arts were funded by the government, has been shifting more and more to private support, and arts organizations have had to adapt.

Despite the trend of dwindling cultural spaces and funding, there have been some encouraging developments in Vancouver's cultural

← **YORK THEATRE**
Located at the foot of
Commercial Drive, the York
is accessible by major transit
and within walking distance
of numerous entertainment
amenities.

scene like the recent revitalization of the York Theatre. Once a beloved
community theatre, the York had become a vacant and ramshackle
building, which had faced more than one threat of demolition. It is now
a beautifully restored, modernized, and operational theatre being used
by a variety of performing arts groups. The reopening of the York Theatre has been a coup for all of Vancouver and its cultural scene.

As recently as 2008, the theatre had been listed by the Heritage
Vancouver Society as one of their "top 10 endangered sites" that the city
was at risk of losing. In a fairly young city like Vancouver, the York
Theatre is historic—a 100-year-old venue with a rich history. The last-
minute rescue of the York Theatre was made even more poignant by
the fairly recent loss of other historic venues in Vancouver, including
the Pantages and Ridge theatres. As Charles Demers, the author of the
play that opened the revitalized York Theatre, told the *Vancouver Sun*,
"It's a thrill that in a city that seems to be losing cultural heritage left
and right—from the Pantages to the Ridge—the York was saved last
minute. We're deeply indebted to everyone who made that possible,
politically and economically. As an artist as well as just being someone
from the neighbourhood I'm super excited to have a venue like this
reopening in the 'hood."

The 1907 Pantages Theatre at Main and Hastings streets was
demolished despite its prominence. It was the oldest-surviving

vaudeville theatre in western Canada and the second vaudeville theatre in North America that was constructed by the famous vaudeville promoter Alexander Pantages, who dreamed of a string of Vaudeville theatres across North America. As deals failed over time to save the Vancouver Pantages theatre, it was finally demolished in 2011 after the roof collapsed due to years of water damage. The story of the Pantages Theatre offers a stark alternative fate for the York Theatre had an innovative cross-sector partnership not stepped in to save it.

In an unprecedented deal between Wall Financial Corporation and the City of Vancouver, the acquisition of the land, renovations, and new construction of the York Theatre were all funded by Wall Financial, primarily in exchange for a heritage density transfer the developer can use on another site. As a result of the deal for the heritage density transfer, the City of Vancouver now owns the York Theatre and leases it at minimal cost to the Vancouver East Cultural Centre, known as "the Cultch". The Cultch is an important cultural institution on the Eastside of Vancouver, and a source of tremendous pride for the neighbourhood. The Cultch features artistic performances that it produces, as well as serves as a venue for other performing arts groups. The York Theatre reopened on December 6, 2013, as part of the Cultch, and its new life as a performance space is just beginning.

The York Theatre originally opened in 1913 as the Alcazar Theatre at 637 Commercial Drive on the Eastside of Vancouver. It was designed by John McCarter, a prominent Vancouver architect of the day. (McCarter and his partner, George Nairne, designed the landmark Marine Building at 355 Burrard Street.) From 1939-1940, the theatre was modified by H.H. Simmonds, another architect with his historical fingerprints on buildings throughout Vancouver, especially theatres. With his renovations, the theatre became representative of the Art

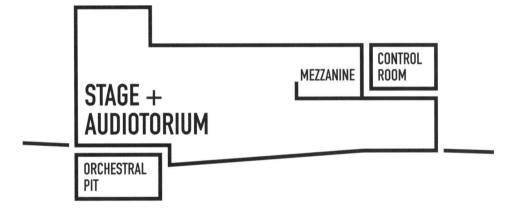

STAGE +
AUDIOTORIUM

MEZZANINE

CONTROL
ROOM

ORCHESTRAL
PIT

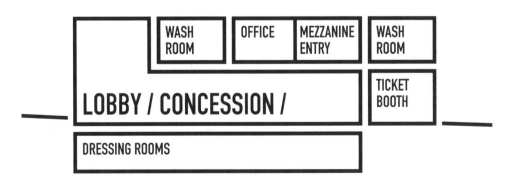

WASH
ROOM

OFFICE

MEZZANINE
ENTRY

WASH
ROOM

LOBBY / CONCESSION /

TICKET
BOOTH

DRESSING ROOMS

PROGRAM DIAGRAM

Deco theatres of that time. (It was this 1940s façade that was preserved by the most recent renovations designed by Henriquez Partners Architects.) By 1940, the theatre became known as the York Theatre, and served as the home for the Vancouver Little Theatre Association for 54 years, allowing them to become one of Canada's oldest continuously operating theatre companies. As a community theatre in Vancouver, it launched many local talents to greater acclaim. The theatre then became a rock and punk concert venue in the 1980s and early 1990s, which showcased bands like Nirvana, Sonic Youth, the Dead Kennedys, and Black Flag. (Gregory Henriquez fondly remembers shows he saw there in his youth). In 1980, it became a theatre for Bollywood films, and then again in the mid-1990s as the notably pink Raja Theatre. The Raja Theatre sign was still visible when the most recent renovations and construction commenced.

The Henriquez Partners' design restored the 1939 Art Deco entrance façade, and preserved the exterior walls of the 1911 theatre. The interior was updated to a 370-seat contemporary theatre with preservation of structural and architectural elements of the original theatre to the extent practicable. The newly revitalized theatre, including a new adjacent addition, was constructed to achieve the equivalent of gold under the LEED rating system. A modern two-storey lobby with a glass front was constructed as an addition to the theatre and was designed to mimic a proscenium arch through which the audience views the performance. Henriquez described the lobby design in an interview with *The Georgia Straight*, "At night when it lights up, you'll see all the people inside the lobby become the actors in a stage set, with spectators being outside on the street. The lobby itself becomes a metaphor for the use, which is the theatre. So it's a piece of urban theatre, which is the idea of the building."

So how did Henriquez Partners come to design this new urban theatre fashioned out of both the historical and modern? After a long history as a performing arts and entertainment space, the York Theatre became vacant. In 1981, Tom Durrie, who lives across from the York Theatre, started the Save the York Theatre Society attempting to intervene when the then owner was threating to demolish the building. (In light of community pressure, it instead became a musical venue and then the Raja Theatre.) At one point when the York Theatre was on the market, the Cultch tried to raise the necessary funds to buy the theatre, but was unable to do so, according to Heather Redfern, the Executive Director of the Cultch.

In the summer of 2008, Durrie saw workmen removing pieces of the theatre and became alarmed that demolition was again imminent. EDG Homes formed a separate entity to purchase the site in 2007 for $952,000, and obtained a building permit to construct a three-storey, five-unit townhouse development on the site. Durrie contacted Redfern and together they enlisted the support of Jim Green, a former city councillor, community activist for the Downtown Eastside, and a supporter of culture and the arts. Green, with his passionate support of the arts and the neighbourhood, was able to convince Vancouver City Council, including the newly elected Vision Vancouver party, that the site had historical significance. The site was not listed on the Vancouver Heritage Register at the time, but the Vancouver Heritage Commission provided support for its historical significance and eligibility for inclusion on the Register. In September of 2008, Green, Henriquez, and the York Theatre allies were able to get a 120-day temporary protection order for the site from City Council to prevent the imminent demolition.

In the four-month reprieve granted by the City, those wanting to save the theatre needed to complete a feasibility study to assess the capital costs to restore it and ensure its long-term operation and viability as a community theatre. In that time, Green was able to reach out to developer Bruno Wall, the President of Wall Financial Corporation, who has developed a strong reputation as a patron of the arts in Vancouver. Wall agreed to help.

Green also enlisted the help of Henriquez Partners, a long-time partner on several community projects, to help with the York Theatre feasibility study. Wall subsequently hired the firm to prepare the design for the renovation when the feasibility study proved the theatre's long-term viability. The plan was that Wall's company would purchase the site for approximately $2 million dollars from EDG Homes and subsequently finance the renovation. Once renovated, the Cultch would operate the new theatre. The proposal was that the entirety of the capital funding needed to construct and renovate the site would be funded by Wall, in exchange for its equivalent value in a heritage density transfer from the City. This critical component to make the deal work was a wild card as it would require the City's approval. At Jim Green's urging, Wall purchased the site in advance of obtaining the City approval for the heritage density transfer in order to ward off demolition. Wall admits, "It was done a bit on a wing and a prayer. We bought the site not knowing whether we'd get City approval to pull this plan off."

In December 2008, Vancouver City Council went against its own staff's recommendation and approved the transaction. Wall accepted the complete financial project cost of approximately $14 million, in exchange for being granted a full transfer of heritage density from the York Theatre. This heritage density transfer allows the bonus area to be applied to a future Wall project, on a site yet to be determined.

(Normally, heritage density can be sold or traded, but in this instance, Wall agreed to only use the density for the company's own projects.) City staff did not want this deal approved because culture is traditionally funded by the federal government in Canada, although now it is more a mix of federal, provincial, and municipal funding. They did not want to set a precedent that the City would solely fund cultural institutions. The City Council took a more pragmatic approach rooted in the ideology that had recently succeeded in getting Vision Vancouver elected: this cultural institution could be saved entirely with heritage density and in a neighbourhood that sorely needs an allocation of more cultural resources. The deal went through.

The City now owns the York Theatre site, which it leased to the Cultch for 60 years. The Cultch contributed $1.8 million in capital funding towards the project and is responsible for all regular and ongoing maintenance under the lease, along with shared capital maintenance with the City. The Cultch operates the site for its own productions, and as Redfern says, it also serves as a "cultural hub" by the Cultch leasing the site to other performing arts groups. Prior to the addition of the York Theatre, the Cultch had two performing spaces at 1895 Venables Street: the Historic Theatre, renovated in 2008, and the newer Vancity Culture Lab (or C-Lab), built in 2008. The York Theatre more than doubles the seats that the Cultch had previously, and provides Vancouver a much-needed performance venue of its size.

Saving the York Theatre involved preserving a historical gem, but it was also a victory for the Eastside of Vancouver, which often views the Westside of Vancouver as the wealth centre that receives more abundant resources. At a press conference announcing the City Council approval for the deal, Mayor Gregor Robertson acknowledged this by saying, "This is undoubtedly going to be a great addition to the north

end of Commercial Drive. We need to be enabling neighbourhoods across the city to have the arts close at hand, and certainly this is a real boost for a part of our city that hasn't perhaps had its share."

Marsha Lederman, a journalist for *The Globe and Mail*, suggests that the reopening of the York Theatre could be the sign of a "cultural watershed moment" for the Vancouver area. She points to the possible new Vancouver Art Gallery (and the cultural institution that may occupy the space it vacates), the Presentation House Gallery moving to a new waterfront space in North Vancouver, the new campus for Emily Carr University of Art + Design on Great Northern Way, the proposed Centre for Art, Architecture + Design in West Vancouver, Michael Audain's new art museum in Whistler, and the Anvil Centre, with a theatre, art gallery, museum, and archives in New Westminster.

In 2014 Henriquez Partners and Wall Financial received a Heritage BC Award of Honour for the rebirth of the York Theatre. Whether this theatre's rebirth will prove to be at the heart of a larger cultural transformation has yet to be seen, but this restored and modernized theatre will provide another important performance space and bring more cultural resources to a part of the city which does not always receive them. The saving of the York Theatre is a true story of collaboration among all sectors. It was saved by the awareness raised by committed activists, a developer with a passion for the arts and an ability to take on risk, an architect able to blend a vision of history and the future, a dedicated cultural organization with the proven ability to operate the York, and an enlightened City able to embrace an innovative deal in order to save a historic theatre and revive an important cultural asset for the city.

It was no surprise that Wall Financial was on the top of the list of developers who might be able to save the York Theatre. The company is a regular supporter of the Vancouver Opera and the Vancouver Symphony Orchestra, and it has also funded community opera programs in the Downtown Eastside. One of Wall's projects, with Macdonald Development, was the Capitol Residences condominium building. The developers received increased density in exchange for constructing $23 million in cultural amenities, including an expansion of the adjacent Orpheum Theatre's backstage area, a rehearsal hall, and the Vancouver Symphony Orchestra music school. (It was no small feat from a construction standpoint to create acoustical separation of a hall used for professional audio recording from the residential building above it.)

The company also has a history of supporting Vancouver's theatre scene. A Wall Financial condominium project in False Creek included a new $14 million facility for the Playhouse Theatre Company. (When the Playhouse Theatre Company shut its doors, Bard on the Beach and the Arts Club Theatre Company took over the theatre space.) Wall Financial also funded the $1.4 million contribution to renovate the Stanley Theatre on Granville Street. This funding represented the City's portion of the expenses, in a cost-sharing arrangement with the provincial and federal governments, and Wall Financial received increased density on its One Wall Centre in exchange. The Arts Club took over the operation after the renovations were completed in 2000.

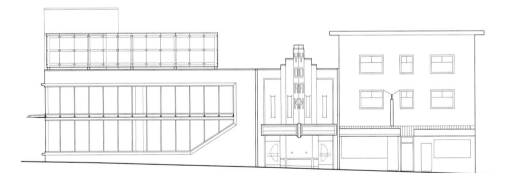

YORK THEATRE
EAST ELEVATION

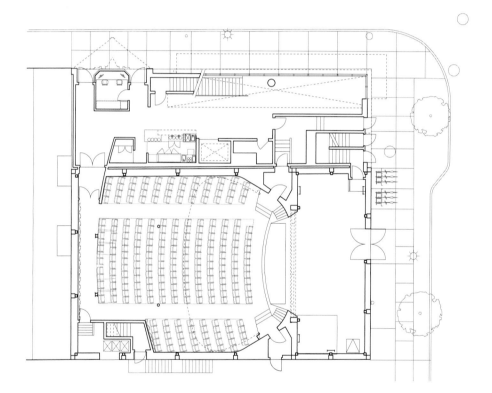

YORK THEATRE
GROUND FLOOR PLAN

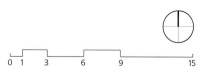

0 1   3   6   9   15

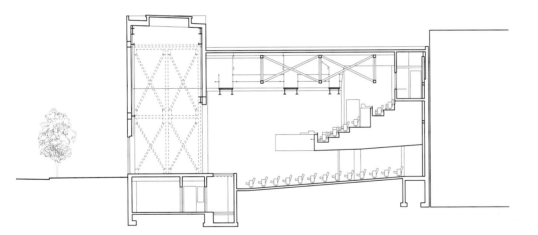

0 1   3   6   9   15

YORK THEATRE
SECTION

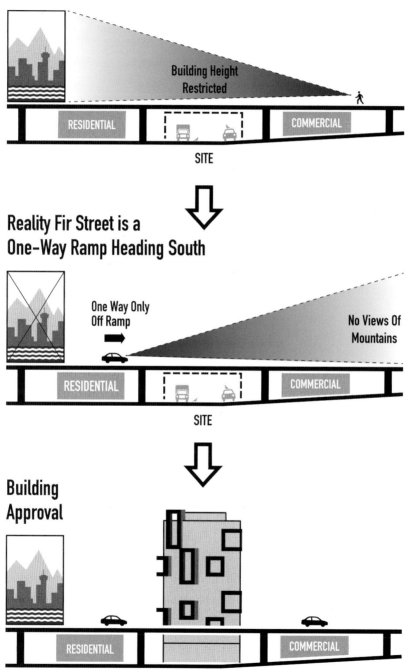

Bridge Head to Protect Mountain Views to the North

Building Height Restricted

RESIDENTIAL

COMMERCIAL

SITE

Reality Fir Street is a One-Way Ramp Heading South

One Way Only Off Ramp

No Views Of Mountains

RESIDENTIAL

COMMERCIAL

SITE

Building Approval

RESIDENTIAL

COMMERCIAL

SITE

Carving Out
Space for Artists
6th & Fir Condominiums

"Affordable studio space for artists has increasingly become a serious problem in Vancouver."

GREGORY HENRIQUEZ

IN THE FALL OF 2013, residents started moving into 6th & Fir, a new 15-storey boutique condominium residence tower by Westbank. Located between the upscale South Granville area to the east and youthful and eclectic Kitsilano to the west, it is part of what City of Vancouver maps call the Burrard Slopes area. The elegant curvilinear tower was designed by Henriquez Partners Architects and is an optical illusion of sorts—from the Fir Street off-ramp of the Granville Street Bridge the tower looks elliptical, but from other points of view it seems orthogonal.

Although architect Gregory Henriquez jokes that the building "essentially designed itself" because of the unique site and its constraints, the joke belies the difficulty in creating a beautiful and workable residential building hedged in by the Granville Street Bridge off-ramp to the west and existing mid-block lower-rise residential sites to the east and north. There was a great challenge in designing the building to minimize the impact on the existing neighbours and to ensure occupants of the new building did not feel bothered by the presence of the bridge off-ramp. For safety reasons, it was also important to minimize possible distractions for drivers.

The City of Vancouver's Bridgehead Guidelines dictate that buildings constructed adjacent to a bridge cannot have a height greater than

← **6TH & FIR**
Located at the corner of 6th Avenue
& Fir Street in the Burrard Slopes
neighborhood of Vancouver.

the bridge deck. This created challenges in developing the site at all. The previous owner of the site, who ultimately sold the property to Westbank, had an earlier development plan that never came to fruition. Westbank's previous architects, Arthur Erickson and Nick Milkovich, designed a building in accordance with the Bridgehead Guidelines, which also was not viable and did not proceed. The combination of the Bridgehead Guidelines, the size of the lot, and the permitted density on the site made it difficult to create an economically viable development.

However, in 2010 a more aggressive argument about the Bridge-head Guidelines from newly hired architect Henriquez, coupled with the ability of Westbank to transfer density to the site from the Wood-ward's Redevelopment, gained some traction with a more receptive City eager to place density where it was perceived that it would be well received. Henriquez argued that the Bridgehead Guidelines were really designed to prevent obstruction of mountain and city views from the bridge itself, particularly as one enters downtown from the Granville Street Bridge. The Fir Street off-ramp, on the other hand, is a curving one-directional southbound off-ramp that faces away from the moun-tains and does not fall within the priorities underlying the policy to preserve vistas from the bridge itself. The City was receptive to this argument especially because there was a strong trade-off to be gained. As Damon Chan from Westbank noted, "It was an evolution by the City. They realized they have to put the increased density somewhere and there was already density in the neighbourhood, so it made sense from that standpoint. It was really a change in priorities by the City."

The tall, slim tower design and its orientation on the site reflected a desire to maximize the views of the Burrard Inlet, to address the proximity of the bridge off-ramp, and also to avoid overshadowing its lower rise neighbors. With the height of the tower, Henriquez Partners was able to sculpt the form of the building which allowed for more light to enter the surrounding green space and to create less shadowing of the existing neighbours. The curved shape helped create distance from the bridge off-ramp and reoriented the units towards views of Burrard Inlet. There is also a wall of bamboo to create a vegetative, visual screen between the residents and the off-ramp for those in the lower units, as well as extensive landscaping in order to make the area around the building green and pleasant for the residents and neighbours. The project's design received acclaim in 2014, winning the Vancouver Urban Design Award for the Best Large Residential Building.

At street-level, YYoga operates a yoga studio in the building's amenity space. Purchasers of units at 6th & Fir received free membership for the first few years of occupancy. Having a yoga studio serves as a local convenience and attraction for residents and neighbours. The constant activity of a yoga studio energizes the street-level retail space.

According to Chan, "These amenity spaces often end up being dead spaces.... And to get a professional operator in there activates traditionally under-utilized spaces in the city." Furthermore, as condominium associations (or "strata associations" in British Columbia) try to save on costs as the years go by, they often cut funding for replacing or upgrading equipment, or for staffing the space. Having a partnership with a commercial entity assures on-going operation and a certain level of quality and maintenance.

Even in a market-rate boutique residential development like 6th & Fir, public amenities are generated under the City of Vancouver's CAC program. As described in more detail in "Urban Planning and

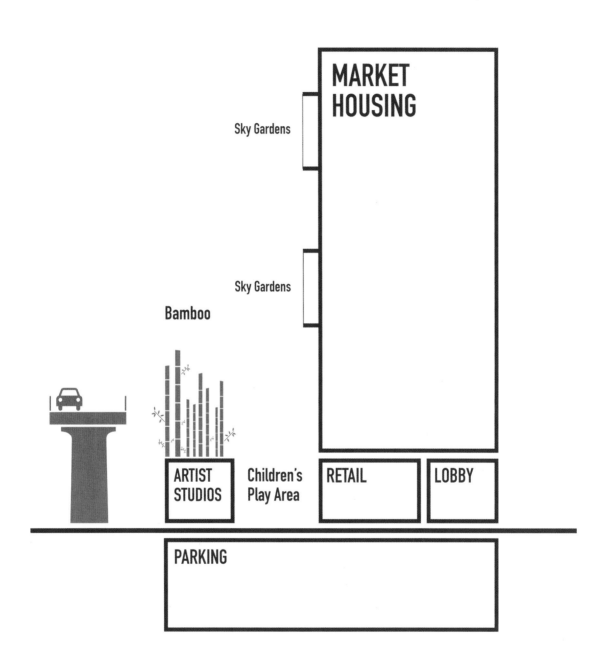

MARKET
HOUSING

Sky Gardens

Sky Gardens

Bamboo

ARTIST
STUDIOS

Children's
Play Area

RETAIL

LOBBY

PARKING

PROGRAM DIAGRAM

Development in Vancouver" starting on page 41, a CAC is a voluntary contribution made by the developer, and the amount and purpose is negotiated between the developer and the City. In the case of 6th & Fir, the City and Westbank negotiated a contribution of $774,000 that would fund an on-site cultural amenity and a nearby neighbourhood park. The on-site cultural amenity, in the form of two artist studios, was transferred into City ownership once the construction was completed by the developer. Under the City's Transfer of Density Policy, the developer also transferred an 8,600 square feet density bonus from the Woodward's Redevelopment to this site, which was valued at $802,000. (For more of a discussion on density transfers, see "Urban Planning and Development in Vancouver" starting on page 41.) This was a move welcomed by the City, which recognized the difficulty of developing on the peculiarly small site without increased density, and wanted the additional density bonus placed on a receiver site where the impact would not be on a great number of people.

The selection of artist studios as a CAC was a deliberate choice by the City—the continuation of an idea from previous development plans that included artist studios. Artists tend to get priced out of neighbourhoods that they help make more attractive and often lose studio space in the redevelopment process. With high real estate prices, there is little rental space appropriate for artists that they can afford within the city. A 2012 study by Hill Strategies found that based on the 2006 census data, Vancouver had the highest concentration of artists per capita. There is fear that artists have been, or will be, driven out of the city due to real estate costs. The City of Vancouver wants to retain its creative class as it views artists as contributing greatly to the cultural scene in the city.

To preserve and enhance this cultural richness, the City is increasing the amount of space available for working artists by encouraging

developers to create such spaces through the CAC program, as well as utilizing City-owned spaces for this purpose. For example, the Artist Live-Work Studio Awards Program is a competition program run by the City of Vancouver, which selects a handful of winning artists who are granted leases for below-market rent for three years. These spaces are a combination of live-work spaces and work-only spaces. The City will lease the artist studios created at 6th & Fir as part of its artist studio program, and these units will increase the number of City-owned units available to be used for art production and to support artists in the city.

In addition to the artist studio program, the City also grants rent-free leases for studio space for artists in parks, park facilities, field houses, and community centres in exchange for community arts-based engagement. The City has also tried to utilize other City-owned spaces to increase art-production space. For example, The Arts Factory is a 21,000-square-foot City-owned industrial space located near Terminal Avenue and Main Street, which has newly renovated production spaces for artists who work with industrial or fabrication processes. The artists can license space and also enjoy the shared amenity spaces. The building is operated by the Arts Factory Society and its anchor tenant is Great Northern Way Scene Shop, which builds sets for arts organizations like Bard on the Beach, the Cultch, and the PuSh Festival.

The City is continuing to look to the CAC program as a way of increasing artist production space, and 6th & Fir serves as an excellent model. Another art-related CAC that has been negotiated is the 10,000-square-foot High Street of the Arts that will be constructed as part of the new 40-storey Tate on Howe condominium project, which is expected to open in 2017 in Yaletown. The High Street of the Arts will be a four-storey glass gallery on Howe Street that will have permanent public art and changing exhibits from artists who will have studios located in this CAC-generated space.

The selection of artist studios as the CAC for the 6th & Fir project has helped the City meet its goal of increasing space dedicated to arts production. The building beside 6th & Fir also contains some artist studios, and Westbank has leased ground-floor retail space in 6th & Fir to art galleries. "Not everything fits in every project, but in this case, the artist studios made a lot of sense," said Damon Chan from Westbank's development team, "and we tried to stay with that theme."

Westbank's CAC of the artist studios and the provision of the funding towards the City's creation of a community park in the neighbourhood adds to the cultural richness of the area as well as making it more livable. Historically, the benefits of CACs do not always stay in the neighbourhood of the project that generates the developer's contribution, but with 6th & Fir, the benefits were retained within the building and community. In September 2013, the City approved the use of a city-owned lot near the 6th & Fir development at the corner of West 6th Avenue and Fir Street for a new community park. The preliminary plans included planting trees in the park and creating seating and a children's playground. Construction was completed in 2014. The park added a much-needed green space in a historically commercial and light industrial neighborhood that is becoming increasingly residential.

The 6th & Fir tower increases the residential density of the area, which aligns with the City's policy of adding residential density in Vancouver's central area and allowing this area to take a substantial share of the expected regional population growth. The 6th & Fir development has helped spur on that process by making the Burrard Slopes area more residential and turning it into a more vibrant, attractive, and identifiable neighbourhood.

6TH & FIR
NORTH ELEVATION

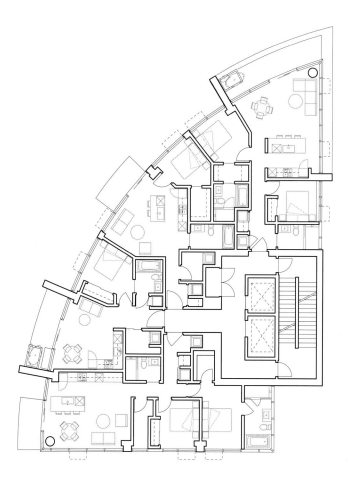

6TH & FIR
FLOOR PLAN LEVEL 4

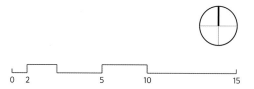

0 2   5   10   15

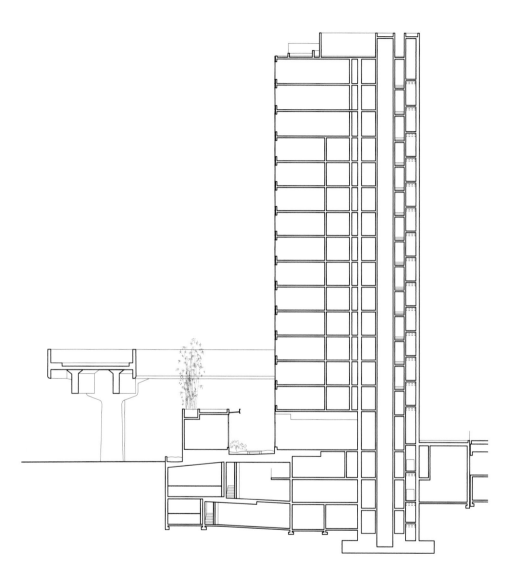

0   2   5   10   15   25

6TH & FIR
SECTION

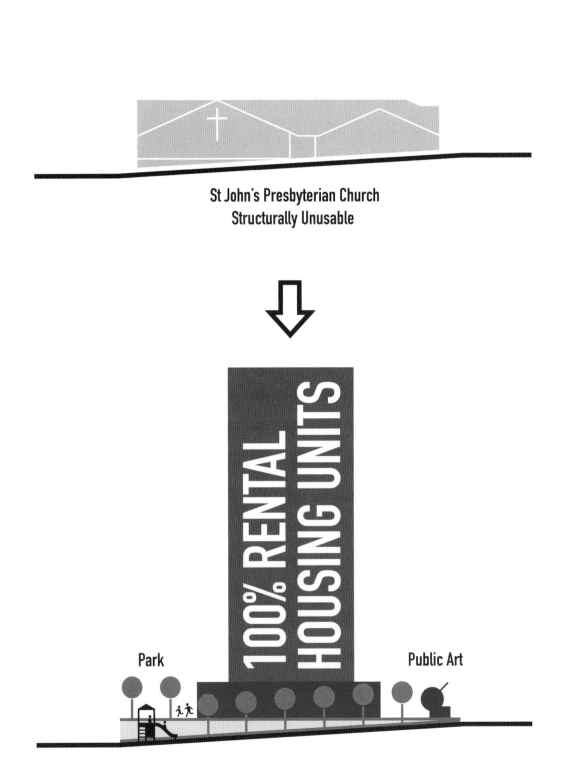

Bringing Rental Density (and Controversy) to the West End
1401 Comox Street

"Rental housing is important in meeting the needs of a diverse population and is vital to a healthy economy. It also allows moderate income households to stay in the city as renter household incomes are typically half that of owners."

RENTAL HOUSING IS an important component of any city's housing stock. According to the City of Vancouver, renter household incomes are typically half that of owners. In addition to increasing the economic diversity of a city, rentals also meet the needs of people in different stages of life: the young, single, seniors, and those who have recently arrived to the city or to Canada, or who are otherwise in transition. However, the high cost of land acquisition in Vancouver in a very competitive real estate market, means that financial models dictate new developments will be condominiums (condos), not purpose-built rentals. The last boom of building rentals was in the1970s, but due to the changing political scene at the federal level, federal tax incentives to build rentals have since been eliminated.

There are many condos that are rented by their owners which adds to the supply of rental apartments in Vancouver and helps keep rental prices much lower than the comparative cost of ownership in the city. However, this is not a complete remedy, as rented condos tend to be more expensive than purpose-built rentals. A 2011 study of the rental market by the Canada Mortgage and Housing Corporation (CMHC) found that on average, a one-bedroom condo rental is 37 percent more

← **1401 COMOX STREET**
Located in West End area of
Vancouver, at the crossroads of
Comox Street and Nicola Street.

expensive than a purpose-built rental. Also, there is uncertainty that the units will remain available as rental units since plans of the owners, the investment environment, and strata rules can all change.

To address the financial challenges inherent in developing new rental projects, Vancouver City Council approved the Short Term Incentive for Rental (STIR) program in June 2009. It was designed as a two-and-a-half year pilot program to grant developers incentives to build rental housing during the economic downturn, offering a mix of incentives including expedited processing of development permits for new rental projects, a waiver of development cost levies, a reduction of the normal parking requirements for development sites, and granting a density bonus.

At the peak of the economic downturn in 2008, it was thought that having the STIR program would encourage the building of rentals. It would potentially create jobs, and test the ability of the City to encourage the building of purpose-built rentals without the assistance of the provincial or federal governments at a time when the construction industry had come to a standstill. Any projects built under the STIR program could not be on sites where existing rental housing would be destroyed for the new project, and the building was required to be rental for the greater of 60 years or the useful life of the building. The STIR program also targeted the development of rentals for moderate-income renters.

One of the first proposed STIR projects was a 100 percent rental development by Westbank and Peterson Investment Group at 1401

Comox Street in Vancouver's West End. The new building is being developed on the site of the former St. John's United Church, which sold its property to Westbank and Peterson with the understanding that the site would be used entirely for rental housing.

In many ways the West End is a prime location for increased density and new rental stock. It is a walkable neighbourhood with many community amenities and with easy access to the Seawall, Stanley Park, and downtown. While it is a commonly held misbelief, the West End is not Vancouver's densest neighbourhood; in fact, it is the fourth most dense. This new building is one of less than two dozen 100 percent rental buildings constructed in the last 40 years in the West End, a neighbourhood where approximately 80 percent of residents rent (compared to 52 percent citywide).

The first development application for the rental project was filed in October 7, 2009, and met with a somewhat unexpected level of controversy. The design went through several iterations, and the process stalled. The plan was finally approved in November 2012, two years after the initial application was filed. The building is called "The Lauren," after the developer's daughter, with a street address of 1061 Broughton Street, and opened in Fall 2014.

The final design features a building that is a bit shorter than the original— slightly less than 200 feet high—with a more sculpted tower and larger setbacks for a greater reduction of shadows on the neighbouring mini-park in front of the nearby Gordon Neighbourhood House. In addition to six ground-level, three-bedroom townhouses for families, there are 180 apartments that range from studios to two-bedroom units. Six units are designated for BC Housing's Shelter Aid for Elderly Renters (SAFER) program, which provides rental subsidies for seniors. The difference between the possible market rate of the unit

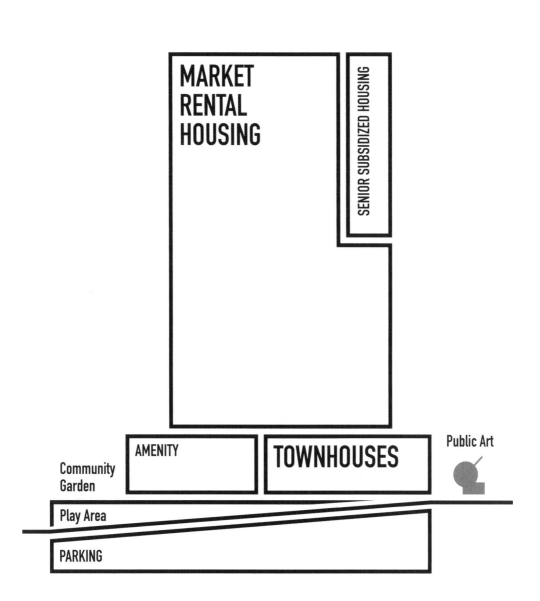

MARKET RENTAL HOUSING

SENIOR SUBSIDIZED HOUSING

AMENITY

TOWNHOUSES

Public Art

Community Garden

Play Area

PARKING

PROGRAM DIAGRAM

and the amount the seniors pay, including the rental subsidy payment from BC Housing, is essentially an ongoing subsidy from the developer. The SAFER units are managed by QMUNITY, British Columbia's human rights nonprofit that serves as a resource center for the lesbian, gay, bisexual, trans, two-spirit, intersex, queer, and questioning community throughout the province, and which provides community outreach, training, education, and advocacy. (The West End currently and historically has a sizeable gay population.)

The development includes a community garden, a play area for children, an amenity space for residents, and extensive landscaping. It incorporates historical components of the St. John's United Church, (originally located on the site) in an effort to preserve part of its history. For example, some of the stained glass and beams have been reused, the original memorial marker for the church was placed outside, and the Roll of Honour for those killed in World War I was incorporated into the new lobby.

When the developers purchased the site from the church, there was a promise to build rentals exclusively and to try to do something that would benefit the community. Rental developments, unlike condo developments, have no Community Amenity Contribution (CAC) required from the developer under the City of Vancouver's current policies, because there is not any increased land value due to rezoning. In spite of this, Westbank/Peterson wanted to voluntarily try to do something for the community. The City proposed that the developer build an amenity space not for residents, but rather a space to be transferred to the City and leased to community groups. The City felt that two longstanding and well regarded organizations within the community would be appropriate possible tenants for the space: the Gordon Neighbourhood House and QMUNITY.

The Gordon Neighbourhood House, which has served as a neighbourhood hub since 1942, runs various community programs, ranging from drop-in care for youth to social activities for seniors. It also runs a food program with an emphasis on the social connections food provides and urban agriculture. The current Gordon Neighbourhood House opened in 1985 and was designed by Richard Henriquez, Gregory's father, with Gregory's help while he was home for the summer before his second year of architecture school. QMUNITY was also considered as a tenant (they will manage the SAFER units in the building).

For both QMUNITY and the Gordon Neighbourhood House, the proposed space in the new building would not be substitute space for their respective existing facilities, but rather new annex space to be used to host community events by either group. However, as the controversy over the project heated up, the project itself, including the community amenity space, was in jeopardy.

Criticisms were wide-ranging. Some people were upset over the historical and cultural loss of the church. There were condo owners who would have preferred more condos over more rentals, especially with the CAC that could have been generated, such as a much-needed renovation to the Vancouver Aquatic Centre. There was a feeling by some that the proposed rental building for moderate-income people was not sufficient to alleviate the affordability crisis and the project should have been geared to people with lower incomes. Some people did not understand the economics of a rental project and why the City's CAC policy did not apply to it and thus did not generate more community amenities.

There were also people concerned with any development and increased density especially in a neighbourhood that has seen little change and development in decades. There was a concern that

development could be a slippery slope and the 1401 Comox project might prompt even more. There were the standard concerns about construction noise, increased traffic, and shadows cast on the neighbours. Many complained about the lack of public process and input. Others complained about the project as an extension of their critiques of the Vision Vancouver party and the view that City Hall had become too "pro-developer." The controversy swirled, as there were protests at City Hall, petitions signed, blogs set up, and groups formed to oppose the development. The WEN Residents Society was formed in 2010, spearheaded by Randy Helten to influence policy decisions and oppose development. Helten is a community and political activist who ran for mayor (and lost) in 2011, and was endorsed by a new civic party, Neighbourhoods for a Sustainable Vancouver.

One of the biggest critiques of the project was that the STIR program itself, as well as the filing of the 1401 Comox initial development application, was done without adequate public consultation and without a current community plan. It was a widely held belief, prior to the emerging controversy over 1401 Comox, that people were concerned about the affordability crisis in Vancouver and that the denizens of the neighbourhood would support the creation of more rental housing stock. Purpose-built rentals in particular would ease the very low vacancy rate, ensure more available rentals in the long term, and possibly bring rental prices down or at least prevent increases.

Architect Gregory Henriquez admits that the development team may have been a bit blind-sided by the level of opposition in the community as they intially believed that a neighbourhood comprised of mostly renters would support more rentals. He admits that they made a mistake in not conducting more public outreach before filing the initial development permit because there was a "misconception by everyone that somehow everyone would see rental as an important thing that needed to happen in the West End." (There were several public meetings and outreach sessions with community groups after the initial application, filing was made and prior to approval by City Council.) The developers made a decision to try to move quickly with the initial application, in part because, at the time, it was feared that interest rates could go up quickly and that even a modest change in interest rates could render the project financially unfeasible.

What exactly happened amid the controversy and how it resulted in a decision to have a rental building without community space for QMUNITY and Gordon Neighbourhood House is not entirely clear. As debate surrounding the new building became more intense, the boards of directors of QMUNITY and Gordon Neighbourhood House became more divided over whether to be associated with the project. At the same time, planners from the City decided to prioritize increased open space. As a result, there is no community annex space in 1401 Comox. Instead there will be a small amenity space for residents, community gardens, and more green space. According to Henriquez, "the very sad part of this story is what could have happened for QMUNITY and Gordon Neighbourhood House."

As more rental buildings come on line due to the STIR program, does the City consider the program a success? According to CMHC data, from 2006-2010 (pre-STIR approved applications), the number of new rental units being developed averaged 150 per year. During the STIR program, the average was 550 units per year. The 2009 "Rental Housing Demand and Existing Supply" study by the City estimated that with current vacancy rates among the lowest in Canada, and with expected population growth, the city needed to add 1,500 new units of rental a year to keep up with a demand, made up of a roughly equal mix of social housing, purpose-built rentals, and secondary rentals (rented condos or laneway housing). From that perspective, the STIR program has been successful in generating new rental units, as well as generating construction employment from the development of those units.

The STIR program, always intended to be a pilot project, ended in December 2011. On May 15, 2012, the learning from the STIR program enabled City Council to adopt its Secured Market Rental Housing Policy, which continues to encourage the development of new rentals through a variety of ways, including the new Rental 100 program. The Rental 100 program includes incentives for developing new rentals and a two-stream process: one for projects not requiring a rezoning, and another negotiated process for those that do.

As for the fate of new space for QMUNITY, their strategic plan for 2013–2015 included the goal of finding a new replacement space for QMUNITY, which will be fully physically accessible to all individuals (unlike their current location), have adequate space for the administrative staff, as well as programming space that will allow more community outreach and programs. The current funding situation for non-profits is extremely challenging. Government funding is not increasing even as cost of living increases, and often comes with restrictions. Canada does not house the same level of foundation giving as the US and Vancouver does not house big corporate headquarters that support cultural and advocacy organizations the way other North American cities do.

This funding crisis, coupled with the high cost of living and real estate prices in Vancouver, make it an impossibility for QMUNITY to buy or develop their own space, so they must rely on cross-sector partnerships—working with the City of Vancouver and developers—in hopes of securing a new location, most likely in a space developed as a CAC in a new development. However, the lack of development in the West End makes this process even more difficult, especially since the organization would greatly prefer to stay in Davie Village, where

QMUNITY and Vancouver's gay community have historical and cultural ties. (The downtown location also helps service its constituents from all parts of the city, since it is conveniently located near transit hubs.) Further complicating the process, historically, at least two developers have shied away from having a gay advocacy organization located in a CAC within their development. "Evidencing," current QMUNITY executive director Dara Parker said wryly, "that our work is never done."

On November 20, 2013, the Vancouver City Council adopted the new West End Community Plan, which recognized the longstanding ties of QMUNITY and its constituents within the West End neighbourhood. The plan also identified a new purpose-built facility in the West End as a priority in order to better support the LGBTQ community. The report also identified the Gordon Neighbourhood House as needing sites for expansion in order to upgrade the facilities, as well as to support more community food programs.

In December 2013, even better news arrived for QMUNITY. The proposed Burrard Gateway Project on Drake Street by the Jim Pattison Group and Reliance Properties is almost one million square feet of commercial and office space and will have over 800 residential units. The rezoning approval contained a CAC of almost $16 million, $7 million of which will be allocated to funding a new space for QMUNITY. The organization is currently actively involved in the public consultation process and is working with the City of Vancouver to identify a new site. "We are delighted that QMUNITY was highlighted as a priority in the West End Community Plan. We have been actively advocating for a new facility that is accessible and large enough to meet the needs of our community programming for 20 years. The new facility will be an inclusive hub for everyone in the queer community, including our allies and neighbourhood supporters," said Parker.

1401 COMOX STREET
NORTH ELEVATION

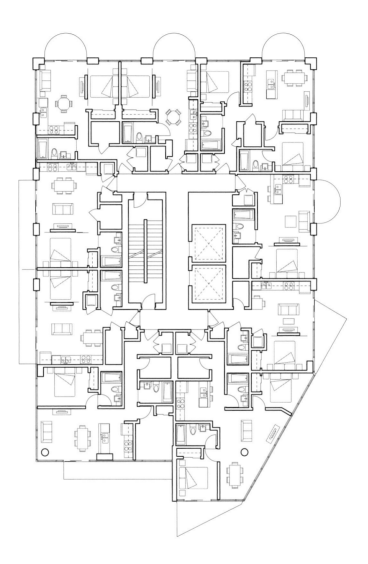

1401 COMOX STREET
FLOOR PLAN LEVEL 8-22

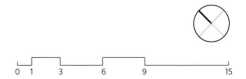

0   1   3   6   9   15

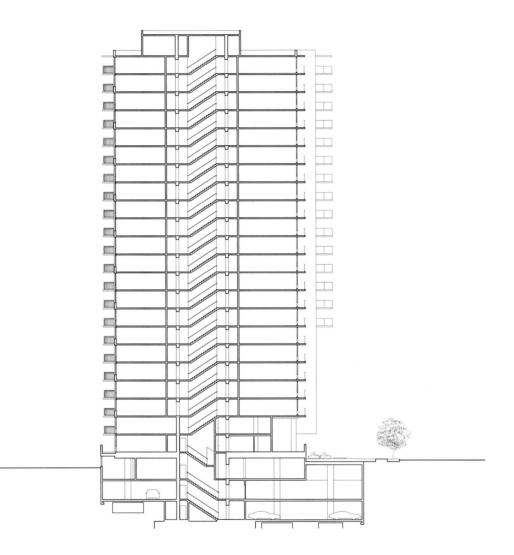

0 2 5   10   15   25

1401 COMOX STREET
SECTION

III. Providing Thought Leadership

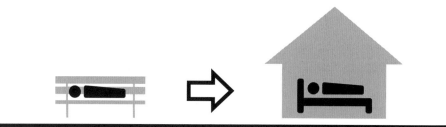

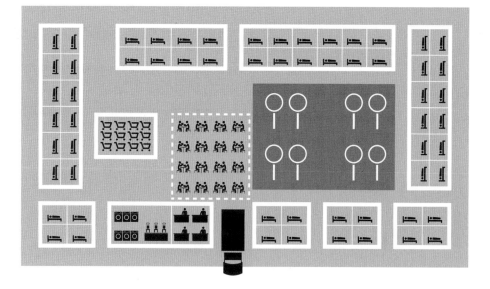

A Creative Step Towards Ending Street Homelessness
Stop-gap Housing

"All of us in the community have long been advocates for permanent housing, but we've gotten to the point where the numbers of homeless are so staggering that one is left wondering if we will ever catch up doing it that way. We don't think we can. We think there has to be a stop-gap measure. And that's what this proposal is."

GREGORY HENRIQUEZ

ON DECEMBER 8, 2008, nearly 400 attendees crowded into the Sunset Community Centre and heard newly elected Mayor Gregor Robertson's inauguration speech, where he pledged to end street homelessness in Vancouver by 2015. Later in the evening, Mike Magee, the Mayor's new chief of staff, was talking to Gregory Henriquez about the issue of homelessness in the city. Magee knew such an ambitious aim by the new administration would require as many ideas as could be generated. He asked Henriquez, "Any ideas?"

Back in his office, Henriquez reflected on his conversation with Magee and decided to take advantage of the slow period the firm was experiencing due to the recession in Vancouver. He grabbed a young architect in his office so they could put their heads together and figure out some ideas on how they might be able to generate a plan that would help alleviate homelessness in Vancouver. The issue has always been a serious and pressing one for Vancouver, but was about to become an issue displayed on the world stage as Vancouver served as the host city for the 2010 Winter Olympics. "With the Olympics," said Henriquez, "you are inviting the whole world to your city. And here we have Canada—an amazing, generous country, and Vancouver—an amazing, gorgeous city, and the fact that our citizens are homeless is a black eye."

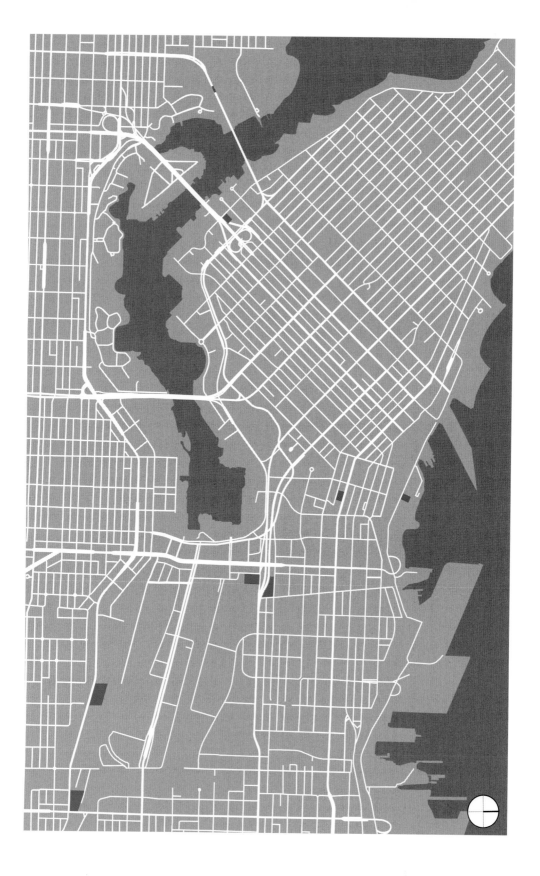

← **STOP-GAP HOUSING**
Potential site locations
selected by PHS.

Henriquez postulated that temporary, stop-gap housing (Stop-gap Housing) could be built inexpensively and provide shelter for Vancouver's estimated 1,500 homeless people (based on a 2008 count) while permanent homes were being developed. (For more discussion on the homelessness problem in Vancouver, please see "The Downtown Eastside and Homelessness in Vancouver" sidebar on page 47.) In the meantime, Henriquez reasoned, people would be off the street, and temporary housing could be done much more cheaply and quickly than permanent housing. With the Olympics looming, the political environment could also be ripe for taking action quickly and making progress on homelessness. The ability to build this housing quickly allowed for a possible solution before the start of the Olympics.

Henriquez decided that they would need a team to develop a strategy and to build and possibly operate the Stop-gap Housing. He promptly made some phone calls. One of Henriquez's first calls was to the leadership of the PHS Services Society (PHS), with whom he had worked on the Woodward's Redevelopment project. As a long time social service provider in the Downtown Eastside working with vulnerable populations, "they have the vigour and knowledge of what needs to be done because of their daily knowledge of people's needs," said Henriquez. He met with Mark Townsend and Dan Small from PHS and discussed the particular needs of Vancouver's homeless population including those individuals who may suffer from mental illness or addiction. They helped develop a design that would be tailored to these particular needs. For example, each unit of the proposed Stop-gap Housing opened to the exterior instead of an interior corridor because an interior corridor could easily become a place of conflict. Each unit would have a bed, desk, and washroom. The encampments on each site would have an inner courtyard for a community gathering space. The second storey above an entry kiosk contained a common area where residents could wash clothes, and a canvas-covered area where meals could be brought in and distributed via food trucks. An area was designated for residents to lock up their carts containing their belongings.

Townsend and Henriquez drove around Vancouver and tried to identify sites where several of the proposed 116-unit villages could be constructed and located. They helped identify eight possible sites that were owned by various levels of government, the Musqueam people, and private entities that might be amenable to leasing the land for a number of years in exchange for property tax relief by the City. Many of these sites were located near areas where homeless people were already sleeping outside—near bridges, the train station, and the Georgia and Dunsmuir Streets viaducts. They tried to select sites that were located near existing support services and in close proximity to transportation.

In addition to PHS, Henriquez quickly assembled a team willing to volunteer their time and services to try to make the idea work. "One thing I learned from this process," revealed Henriquez, "is how many people care and are willing to help if you are willing to pick up the phone and ask for help." Henriquez called Ian Gillespie, the president of Westbank, who offered to act as the developer and to arrange the financing as needed. Britco, a local builder that makes prefabricated modular units often used to house workers at remote sites within Canada, offered to work up specifications for modular units in

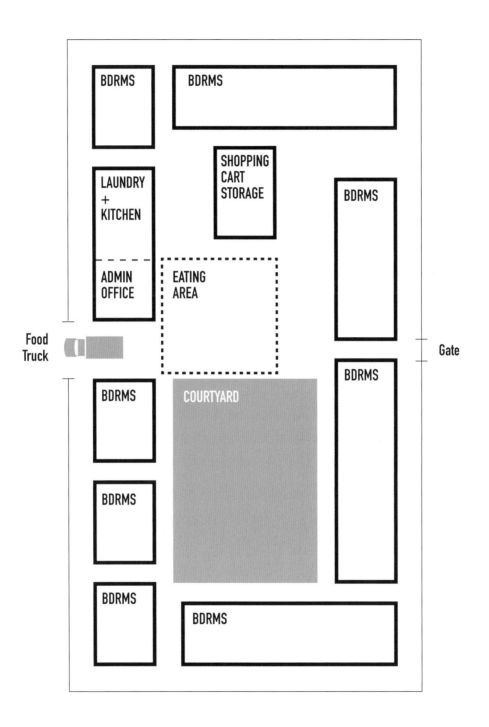

BDRMS

BDRMS

SHOPPING CART STORAGE

LAUNDRY + KITCHEN

BDRMS

ADMIN OFFICE

EATING AREA

Food Truck

Gate

BDRMS

COURTYARD

BDRMS

BDRMS

BDRMS

BDRMS

PROGRAM DIAGRAM

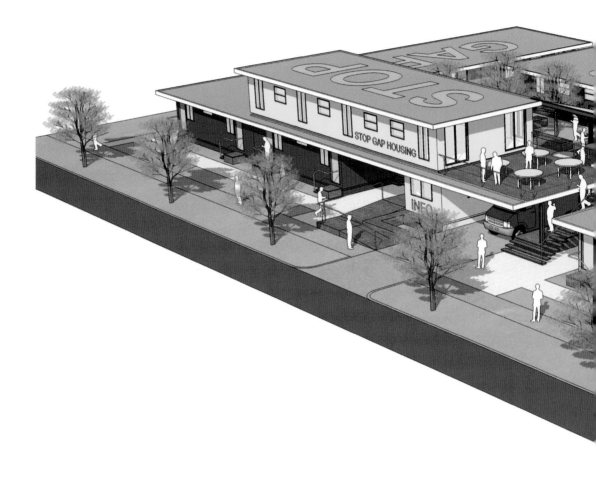

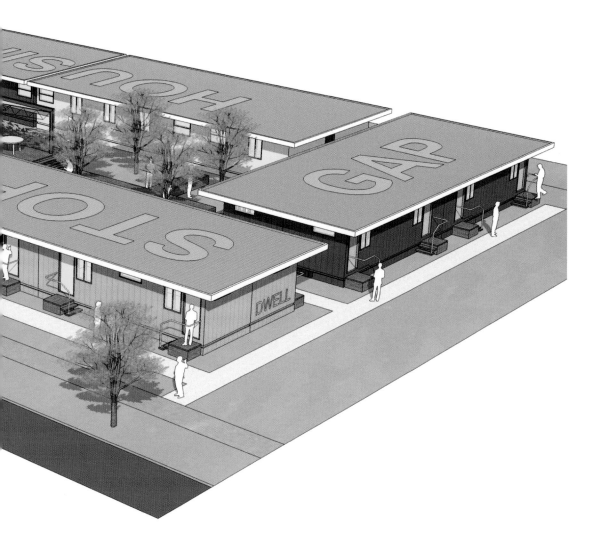

response to Henriquez's design. LMDG Building Code Consultants gave advice on how to build the units in a fashion that could be done quickly with minimal permitting. Haebler Construction and Integral Group helped figure out the capital costs for the site services that would be required. If BC Housing could be brought on board to fund the project and the operations, PHS could serve as an experienced and capable operator. Subject to securing the sites and government funding, a team able to build and operate the Stop-gap Housing was now in place.

The beauty of the Stop-gap Housing proposal was that it could be constructed very quickly and homeless people could be off the street and in temporary housing while more permanent solutions were being constructed. Another benefit was that the Stop-gap Housing could be constructed at a fraction of the cost of permanent housing. The cost estimates were about $50,000 per unit, including furnishings, which may seem expensive but, considering how stabilizing housing can be for vulnerable people, this cost could actually represent a savings for taxpayers. According to a 2008 study by Simon Fraser University's Centre for Applied Research in Mental Health and Addiction, taxpayers spend an average of $55,000 per year for medical, social, and correction services for each homeless person in BC. This cost is not to house them, but rather just to react to and maintain the homeless condition of these individuals.

Even among the Stop-gap Housing team, there was consensus that the preferred solution was permanent housing, and that Stop-gap Housing could be just that: a stop-gap measure before permanent solutions could be obtained. Liz Evans from PHS said, "This was a very doable and very innovative idea. We weren't saying that people should live in Britco trailers forever as a dignified way of living. We called it

Stop-gap Housing intentionally because we didn't want people to think we thought this was a permanent housing solution." However, the temporary nature of the housing was a problem for some critics. There was a concern that building temporary housing would alleviate the pressure on government to build permanent housing. Some people, like community activist Jim Green, felt that the homeless should be in permanent housing that provides a greater level of dignity. Others were worried that temporary has a way of becoming permanent and that what was intended to be temporary housing would end up being dilapidated housing used past the point for which it was intended. There were disagreements, even within the housing advocacy community, as to whether creating these communities would be beneficial in highlighting the problem—making the size and existence of the homeless population more visible and undeniable—or whether it was institutionalizing poverty and a form of internment of poor people.

The capital costs were criticized because that funding could be put towards permanent housing, instead of towards temporary housing that still would not result in permanent housing. But it was really the ongoing operational costs that daunted government funders and possibly killed the idea. These ongoing operational costs were estimated at $750,000-$1,000,000 per year, per site. Each of the eight proposed sites would have provided approximately 116 units. For $8 million dollars or less, there could have been 928 homeless people housed each year in the Stop-gap Housing. However, BC Housing viewed this proposal as more of an experimental idea. They viewed it as too costly and not part of their policy mandate. Without provincial funding, the proposal was doomed.

Ironically, an even more temporary solution may have been perceived as more politically palatable. Shelters can be assembled and dissembled relatively quickly in existing buildings which makes them very cost effective, flexible, and mobile. Shelters are not perceived to be as politically risky as other options because there is not the same level of policy commitment due to their impermanence. There is not the concern that shelters will replace a permanent housing solution, nor is there the same fear of an indefinite ongoing housing operational subsidy.

As much as the proponents of Stop-gap Housing believed the zeitgeist of improving the city in anticipation of the Olympics could propel political progress on the homelessness issue, there was another political reality that was hard to overcome. Evans believes that Canadians are sympathetic to the plight of the homeless: "Generally, I think it [the issue of homelessness] falls on supportive ears most of the time. Canadians believe that people who are on welfare and are really struggling do deserve a home." At the same time, she noted, the dissension starts when discussing where that home will be. There is a "Not in My Back Yard" problem (so-called NIMBYism), where the community objects to having something perceived as undesirable or dangerous in their community. This issue plagued the Stop-gap Housing proposals when certain communities learned that there was a site in their neighbourhood that might be considered for one of these Stop Gap Housing communities. This reaction has also posed a problem for the City's Housing Emergency Action Team (HEAT) shelters. In fact, this issue has inspired Pivot Legal Society, which advocates for "homes for all" as part of its mission, to introduce a "Yes in my backyard! [YIMBY] Toolkit" to spread the word about how to make communities more inclusive and supportive.

It is clear even years after the Stop-gap Housing proposal, its proponents are disappointed that there are still homeless people on the street and that even the pressure of hosting the Olympic games was not enough to catalyze political will. Dan Small from PHS noted, "With the Olympics, it was the ultimate opportunity to get everyone under the same tent talking about these issues." With some time for context, Henriquez admitted, "When this started out, it seemed like such a simple idea. I couldn't believe it hadn't been tried before. But then what I learned is that there are all kinds of political forces that didn't really see the proposal as credible…. I am more of a dreamer than I thought I was. I thought I was being a pragmatist but I realized that as practical and reasonable as the idea appears, I was being politically naïve."

It is not all grim news, however. Since the Stop-gap Housing proposal, there has been progress made in Vancouver towards permanent housing for the homeless. A partnership between the City of Vancouver and the Province of British Columbia has resulted in the commitment by the City to contribute 14 sites for the construction of permanent housing, which will be funded by BC Housing. Vancouver Coastal Health and the Streetohome Foundation are also participating in this partnership, which will result in 1,200 new supportive housing units. In July 2015, BC Housing announced that the tenth building of the proposed fourteen projects had opened for occupancy. While new permanent housing was being built, the City and BC Housing have operated additional winter-month shelters to protect homeless people from the cold weather and to try to connect them to services. According to the City, in the last five years (as of late 2013) over 500 people have transitioned from these Winter Response Shelters into permanent housing. While the progress may be slow for those still living on the street, there has been tremendous progress made in adding permanent housing for the homeless in Vancouver.

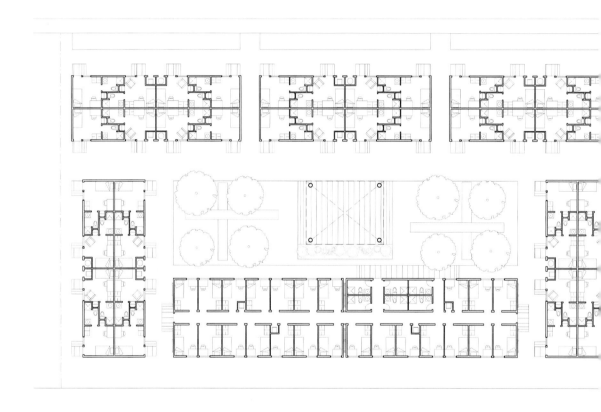

0   2   5   10   15   25

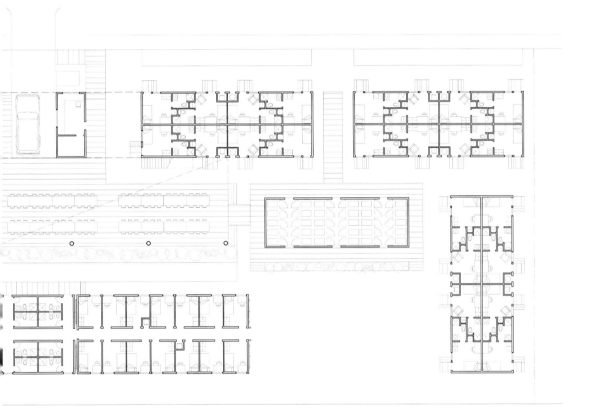

STOP-GAP HOUSING
GROUND LEVEL PLAN

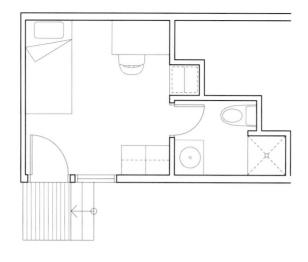

Suite with Bathroom
and External Access —140sf

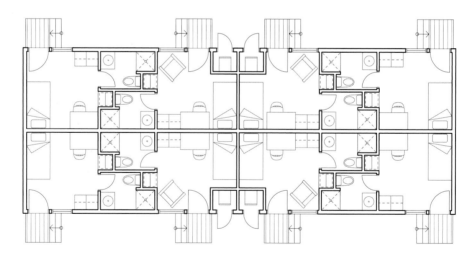

Typical Module Layout—8 Units

STOP-GAP HOUSING
TYPICAL FLOOR PLAN

0   1   2   5   10

BURRARD BRIDGE

BURRARD BICYCLE BRIDGE

Wading into the Debate over Debate over Bike Lanes

A Passerelle for Vancouver

"Equal to design competitions are targeted individual acts of initiative.... Architects have an incredible ability to illustrate ideas and should be actively participating in meaningful civic dialogue."

GREGORY HENRIQUEZ

MANY PLACES IN the world have passerelles—footbridges that usually span bodies of water and connect landmarks and cultural sites. From Buenos Aires to Brisbane, Amsterdam to London, these bridges have become iconic parts of their respective cities and have become destinations for residents and tourists alike. The London Millennium Footbridge is a classic example. The 370-metre pedestrian suspension bridge spans the River Thames and links the Tate Modern, the Bankside Gallery, and the Globe Theatre in the Bankside area with the City of London School and St. Paul's Cathedral on the London side. In Canada, Winnipeg has the Esplanade Riel over the Red River, and in 2012, Calgary opened the Peace Bridge spanning the Bow River, which was designed by Santiago Calatrava. In the Vancouver area, the Capilano Suspension Bridge shows off the breathtaking natural beauty of the region from dizzying heights. Should not the city of Vancouver, with its downtown situated on a peninsula apart from the rest of the city, and with its worldwide allure for tourists, be a natural location for a passerelle?

When Mayor Gregor Robertson was elected in 2008, he set out to achieve one of his campaign promises to make Vancouver the greenest

city in the world. In 2011, the City of Vancouver adopted this highly ambitious goal and created the Greenest City 2020 Action Plan to try to achieve it by 2020. An avid cyclist, the mayor also wanted to promote more cycling within Vancouver, which would help reduce the reliance on cars and help reach carbon reduction targets. Having fewer cars on the road would also help reduce the ever-increasing traffic gridlock which afflicts the city.

City of Vancouver staff immediately set about improving bicycle lanes, including introducing separated lanes for enhanced safety. One main arterial of focus was the Burrard Bridge, which links peninsular downtown Vancouver with Kitsilano, the rest of the western portion of the city's neighbourhoods, and the University of British Columbia. The City believed by improving access and safety for bicycles on the Burrard Bridge, it would increase the amount of cyclist commuting, particularly to downtown.

Several proposals were examined. The first set of possible options included modifying the structure of the existing bridge, either by widening the bridge deck by building along the side of it or constructing a new deck below the traffic deck on the underside in the trestles originally designed to carry street cars. Both modification options were considered expensive and not without challenges. Widening the bridge deck would require closing lanes for construction and was estimated to cost roughly $30 million, not including the approximated $30 million already required for seismic updates and upgrades to the bridge, which were required regardless of any further modifications.

The underside option would possibly impact traffic less during construction, but there were concerns about the height and its impact on boats, triggering the involvement of the federal government under the Navigable Waters Protection Act.

The second set of options included various configurations of using the existing sidewalks and traffic lanes for a mix of cars, bicycles, and pedestrians. In May 2009, Vancouver City Council ultimately selected an option to use as a pilot project, which included reserving the western sidewalk for pedestrians only (walking in either direction), the eastern sidewalk for bicycles headed from Kitsilano to downtown, and the western curb lane for bicycles headed from downtown to Kitsilano. This configuration left five lanes of car traffic instead of six, with three northbound and two southbound lanes. Many residents of the Westside of Vancouver opposed the plan as they were furious and fearful that taking away even one lane of traffic would impact traffic too much. Others, like Lisa Slakov of the Vancouver Area Cycling Coalition, criticized the plan for not doing enough for cyclists and asserted there should have been a dedicated bicycle lane in both directions, which would also leave the sidewalks for pedestrians. Although in an interview with BC Living magazine, she acknowledged, "It's a difficult political decision for Council to make [to do] any lane trial reallocations, and from that perspective we really appreciate the fact that they're moving forward."

As the temporary six-month pilot project was being presented, some wondered, *what about a third option of a new permanent bicycle and pedestrian only bridge spanning False Creek?* Intrigued by the idea, architect Gregory Henriquez of Henriquez Partners, teamed up with structural engineer C.C. Yao from Read Jones Christoffersen, and the MMM Group for their bridge expertise, to design a possible pedestrian and bicycle bridge for the city of Vancouver. The proposed design

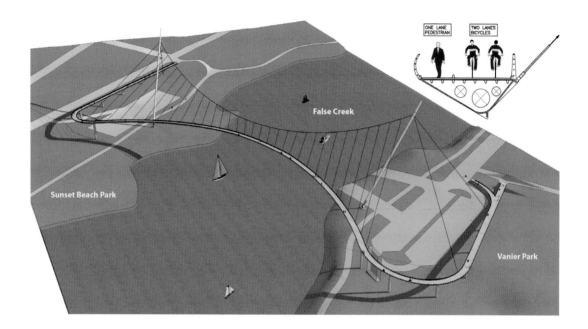

ONE LANE
PEDESTRIAN

TWO LANES
BICYCLES

False Creek

Sunset Beach Park

Vanier Park

released in July 2009 was for a 15-metre-wide bridge with one lane for pedestrians and two lanes for bicycles (one for each direction). The curving bridge deck would be steep enough to allow sailboats to pass beneath it.

In an interview with *The Vancouver Sun*, Henriquez described his vision, "The [curved] design allows for a longer bridge and ramp access, and a more graceful one. It's meant to be a poetic interpretation of a traditional suspension bridge. It's modern and simple like the sail of a boat and is meant to contrast the existing heritage Burrard Bridge, which is neoclassical." The asymmetrical suspension cables, from the eastern side of the bridge only, would allow what Henriquez called "unimpinged ocean views to the west". The bridge would span from Sunset Beach Park over False Creek to Vanier Park, and connect one section of Vancouver's popular bicycle and pedestrian lanes along the Seawall to another.

The permanent solution proposed by Henriquez's design was estimated to cost approximately $45 million. Many critiques of the plan focussed on this cost, regardless of what people thought about the design. Some liked the design and enjoyed the idea of creating an elegant and iconic structure that would be a draw for tourists as passerelles have been in other world cities. Others were quick to point out that passerelles are usually connectors of important cultural sites, whereas in this instance there were only beaches and the linkage of the Seawall. (Frances Bula, noted journalist and city commentator, suggested in her blog that in order for the proposed bridge to do what the Millennium Bridge did for London, it should be anchored by cultural sites and suggested, perhaps tongue-in-cheek, that one end be the new location of the Vancouver Art Gallery.) Some worried about the environmental impact on the beaches.

Some considered it a forward-looking option that could become a critical part of Vancouver's movement towards a low-carbon future by encouraging less reliance on cars. It was a contentious issue even among cyclists. Some cyclists were thrilled about the investment in a permanent bridge for cyclists, both as a practical matter and as a symbolic one. Other cyclists were deeply critical of the proposed passerelle, saying that it was too circuitous with the long on-ramps and off-ramps and too far west to serve as a realistic commuting route.

In any event, the City pursued the Burrard Bridge bicycle lanes as its more immediate policy solution, and stopped examining a more permanent option for at least the time being. (The City would not have been committed to Henriquez's design had it decided to pursue a more permanent option, or does so in the future. The City could select a winning design from a design competition, in which all architects, including Henriquez Partners, could participate.) According to Henriquez, the intention of his design was to show that a permanent bridge could be an attractive and viable option and to bring that option into the dialogue about wider possible policy solutions. It was, he says, "an individual act of initiative," and meant to engender civic discussion.

He is not the only architect who has created and released design proposals intended to futher public discussion and encourage greater civic engagement. In another local example, architect Bing Thom opposed a possible move of the Vancouver Art Gallery, believing that its current historical and centrally located site is the proper place for one of the city's preeminent cultural institutions. He favoured the VAG focussing on renovations rather than a move. When interviewed by *The Vancouver Sun*, Thom said, "We don't want to hollow out the centre of city. Vancouver is strong at the edges, near the water, but we desperately need something at the centre. The art gallery is the visible symbol of our culture and it should be at the heart." When a move by the Vancouver Art Gallery appeared to be progressing, Thom created a vision of how the current site could be utilized by designing an ambitious plan for a Vancouver Concert Hall and a reenergized public square.

In April 2013, in spite of such opposition, the City granted a 99-year lease at Larwill Park for the construction of a new purpose-built facility for the Vancouver Art Gallery. Subject to successful fundraising for the new building, the Vancouver Art Gallery will move. Thom continues to believe the central site and square should be preserved for a cultural facility. Other museums have expressed interest in moving to the Georgia Street location, but as of early 2016, the fate of the current Vancouver Art Gallery site remains unknown.

Architects and the design community have an important role to play in civic discussion, particularly with respect to development and creating community within a city. They can give form to ideas, allowing people to envision what a new built environment would look like. The civic debate engendered by the design community can have its own tensions and differing viewpoints. Just as Henriquez believed a new passerelle would enhance Vancouver overall, Thom might argue that the edges of Vancouver near the water are strong enough and that more attention should be paid to the centre. Even this possible disagreement on the best path forward for the city supports what Henriquez believes: architects have an ethical commitment to be dedicated to the community where they are located and to play an active role in civic affairs. Architects, especially local ones, should continue to engage in that civic dialogue with their respective viewpoints. "This isn't about prioritizing trying to win a design competition in Seville—this is proposing local solutions and ideas for the community where you live," says Henriquez.

Henriquez does not think that this is an exclusive role for the design community to play but rather an active role to be taken along with other engaged citizens, "There is a huge desire, you can see from the community plans the City is undertaking, by people to get involved in the process of defining the vision of our city. Everyone has a role to play from the average citizen to developers and those involved in the design industry, activists, NGOs [non-governmental organizations], the media . . . all people have a role to play."

Judging from any letters to the editor page on an average day, the dialogue among Vancouverites debating the right balance and prioritization of car traffic versus pedestrians versus cyclists (and the safety issues of all three) will continue. Meanwhile, the 2009 Burrard Bridge bicycle lane trial resulted in a permanent allocation of a bicycle lane configuration. The concern of a horrific traffic apocalypse failed to materialize, and bicycle ridership is up.

According to the City's statistics, in 2013 there were 35,000 bicycle trips a month on the Burrard Bridge, during the coldest months of December and January, up to a peak of 161,000 trips in July. By July 2014, there was a new record set: 195,000 trips. Unlike the 1996 pilot program that was quickly abandoned as traffic snarled and public opinion soured, the 2009 pilot program seems to have been a success, or at least accepted by Vancouverites. Cycling has increased in popularity, both in terms of prioritizing the development of cycling infrastructure and number of trips made by bicycle. According to the City of Vancouver, trips by bicycle over the Burrard Bridge in June of 2015 showed an increase of 28 percent over trips taken in June 2014. The City of Vancouver, with its ambitious low-carbon plan, and the vocal, engaged denizens of Vancouver will continue to debate all forms of transportation and necessary infrastructure. As this debate rages on, it will continue to shape and reshape Vancouver.

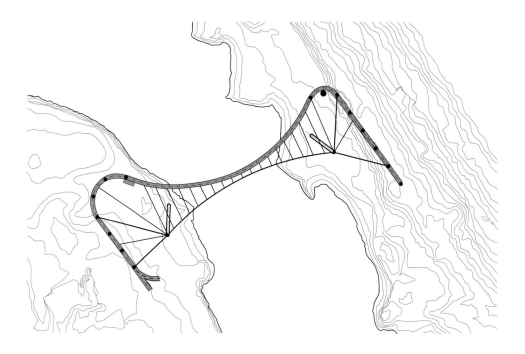

BURRARD BICYCLE BRIDGE
SITE PLAN

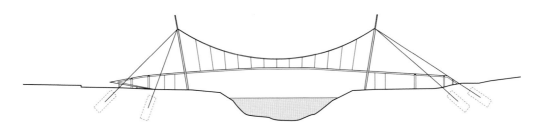

BURRARD BICYCLE BRIDGE
ELEVATION

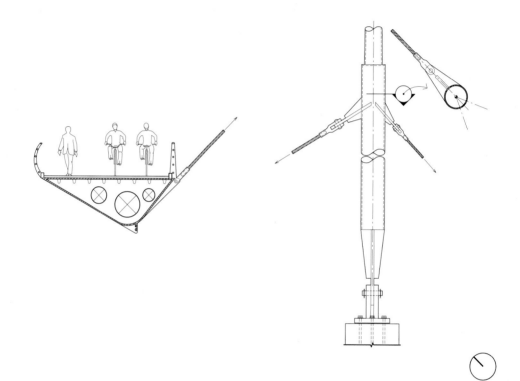

BURRARD BICYCLE BRIDGE
SECTION

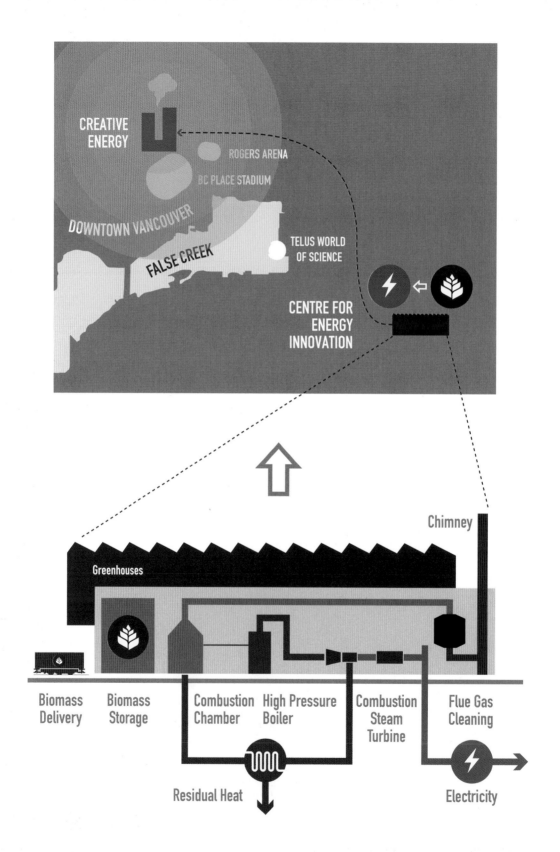

CREATIVE ENERGY

ROGERS ARENA

BC PLACE STADIUM

DOWNTOWN VANCOUVER

FALSE CREEK

TELUS WORLD OF SCIENCE

CENTRE FOR ENERGY INNOVATION

Chimney

Greenhouses

| Biomass Delivery | Biomass Storage | Combustion Chamber | High Pressure Boiler | Combustion Steam Turbine | Flue Gas Cleaning |

Residual Heat

Electricity

A Visionary Developer Sees Beyond LEED for Greater Sustainability
Creative Energy

"I think we have lost the idea that we are not in it [this world] just for ourselves but we are in it to build a better community for the longer term . . . . We have so many opportunities to do more, and we need to take advantage of them."

IAN GILLESPIE

IN 2009, MAYOR Gregor Robertson's Greenest City Action Team began planning how to make Vancouver the most sustainable city in the world by 2020. The City of Vancouver's Greenest City 2020 Action Plan (the GCAP) became a roadmap for how this lofty goal could be achieved. The City admits that it is an ambitious plan—one that will require the deployment and cooperation of all sectors of society to accomplish. Becoming the most sustainable city in the world will necessarily involve various levels of government, the private sector, and non-profit organizations. An example of the private sector taking bold steps towards greater sustainability in Vancouver is a recent undertaking by prominent real estate developer Ian Gillespie of Westbank. One of his companies, Creative Energy Canada Platforms Corp. (Creative Energy), is now the owner of a utility, Central Heat Distribution Ltd. (CHDL), which operates the CHDL steam plant at 720 Beatty Street in Vancouver.

Through Creative Energy, Gillespie is developing a number of strategies on how to bring greater sustainability to Vancouver. One way is through district energy opportunities. Another is through a fuel switch from natural gas to a renewable source at the CHDL steam

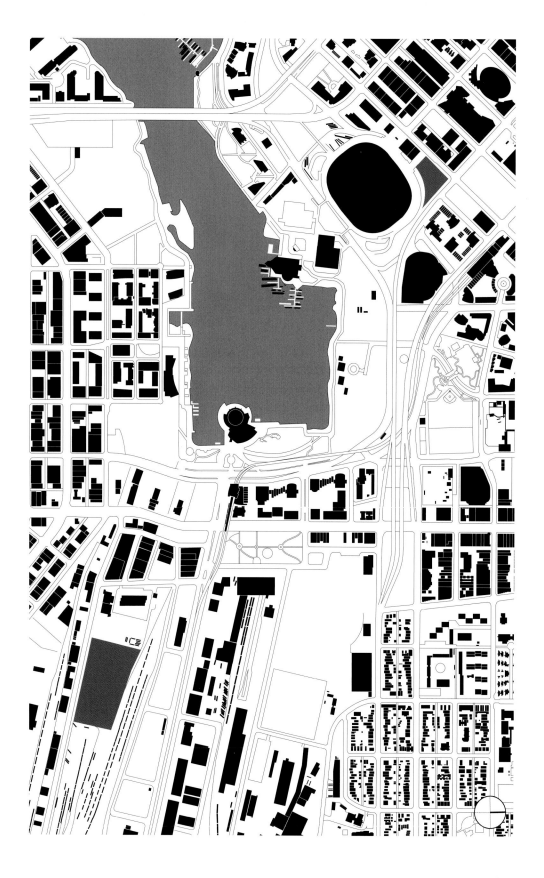

← **CREATIVE ENERGY**
The property is bounded by
Beatty Street, the Georgia
Viaduct, and Expo Boulevard.

plant, which the company is investigating. Meanwhile, Creative Energy is planning on upgrading the distribution system of the CHDL steam plant to a more efficient hot-water system, and expanding its service areas. Envisioning even greater efficiencies citywide, Gillespie is brainstorming with the City about how Vancouver's Dedicated Fire Protection System might be used as a dual-purpose system for both emergency preparedness and as an ambient loop to capture more energy.

This first strategy—district energy systems—is where residential and commercial users of energy get their heating (and/or cooling) from a centralized plant, which provides efficiency over individual systems, flexibility to make large scale changes, and more localized control. This avoids each building on the system needing its own equipment such as furnaces, boilers, chillers, or air conditioners. A current example in Vancouver is the Academic District Energy System at the University of British Columbia, where its steam system is currently being converted to a more efficient hot water system. When completed, this system will heat over 130 buildings. In general, shared infrastructure can have tremendous benefits for cities. This can be on a large scale, like district energy systems or on a smaller scale, like car-sharing programs such as Zipcar and car2go. Shared infrastructure is a cost effective and more sustainable way of using invested capital to provide the infrastructure services cities need.

In addition to district energy systems, Creative Energy is examining the possibility of a fuel switch from natural gas to a renewable source at the CHDL plant. According to an article by Kevin Griffin in *The Vancouver Sun* (February 19, 2014) about this fuel switch possibility, the CHDL plant produces 70,000 tonnes of greenhouse gases a year, and a City of Vancouver report identifies a possible fuel switch at CHDL as the single greatest opportunity for reducing the greenhouse gas emissions in Vancouver. The fuel switch would achieve the equivalent of taking more than 14,000 cars off the road each year. The current carbon footprint of Vancouver, while better than many other major North American cities, is not at a level that can be considered sustainable, and energy innovation is a necessary ingredient in getting Vancouver to a more sustainable future.

The $32 million purchase of CHDL by Creative Energy was approved by the British Columbia Utilities Commission on November 21, 2013, and the acquisition became final 120 days after the regulatory approval. The acquired plant has 242 megawatts of gas-fired boilers and approximately 13 kilometres of steam distribution mains throughout downtown Vancouver. It provides heat to over 210 buildings in the downtown core, including residential and office buildings, hotels, and St. Paul's Hospital. It also serves notable cultural institutions like the Queen Elizabeth Theatre, the Vancouver Public Library Central Branch, and its stadium neighbours, BC Place and Rogers Arena.

A major step for Creative Energy will be upgrading the plant's distribution system in order to convert it from steam to hot water in expanded service areas. A hot-water distribution system is a much more efficient conveyor of heat, because less heat is lost than with the high temperatures required of steam. CHDL was formed in 1968 to create a district energy system to more efficiently provide the downtown core with heat because the buildings connected to the system would not need their own boilers and such a heating system would also

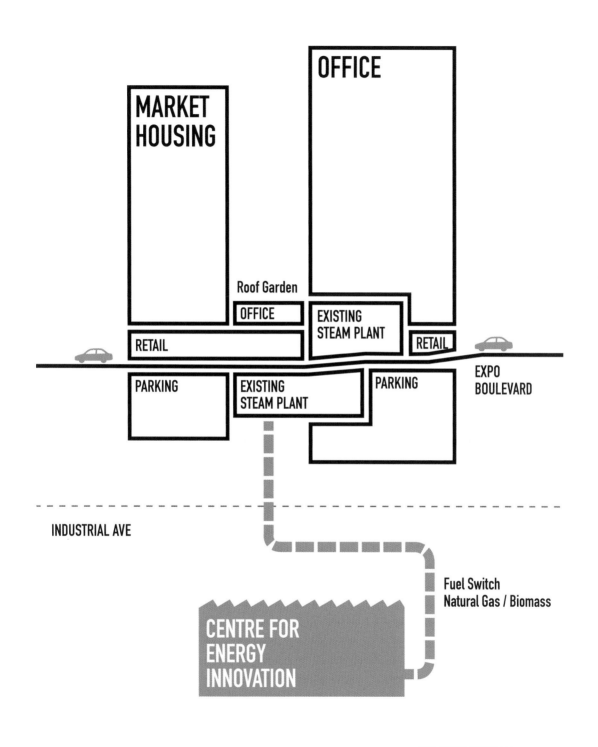

PROGRAM DIAGRAM

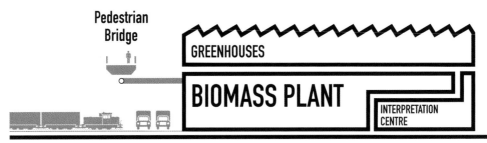

Pedestrian Bridge

GREENHOUSES

BIOMASS PLANT

INTERPRETATION CENTRE

Biomass Train + Truck Delivery Route

CREATIVE ENERGY

reduce the amount of pollution in the downtown area. Converting to an even more efficient hot-water distribution system would result in an immediate reduction of carbon emissions in the downtown core due to the approximately 210 buildings that would be connected to this renovated distribution system.

If this *en masse* building conversion can be achieved, the carbon reductions would be rapid and with a magnitude which dwarfs the increased efficiencies that could be achieved by newly constructed buildings alone. Furthermore, this could be a critical component to even greater sustainability in Vancouver's future. The hot-water distribution system is more compatible with heat recovery between buildings and with using more renewable energy sources if the plant goes through a fuel switch process in the future. In the more immediate future, Creative Energy is in discussions with the City of Vancouver about expanding the CHDL distribution system to connect to major new expansion areas like the South Downtown/Yaletown area and the North False Creek area. The possibility of expansion to other areas of the city is also being studied.

Exploring low-carbon energy districts is very compatible with the City's green building strategy. The City now requires a LEED gold certification for any new rezoning. Since the LEED rating system requires optimization of energy, the low-carbon and renewable energy benefits of district energy systems could help developers meet these requirements and be more efficient than trying to meet these requirements with on-site strategies for each development. Part of Creative Energy's vision of the future is that the City could develop a system that grants developers the ability to take advantage of LEED bonus points resulting from low-carbon district energy systems (like the CHDL system after the fuel switch), and that this cost savings in achieving LEED points could be channeled into helping fund the development of even more alternative technologies and renewable energy sources. Currently, Westbank is working on a project where they are attempting to get the district energy system certified now as achieving certain LEED points based on the system design before it is actually completed. This would allow any developer to receive LEED points towards their building if that building is built, such that it will be capable of connecting to the low-carbon system when it comes on-line in the future.

The acquisition of CHDL made Creative Energy the owner of approximately 77,000 square feet of land at the site of the plant and an adjacent parcel. One parcel is zoned commercial as part of the downtown district and the other parcel is an anomaly with a 1.0 FSR. Any potential development of the land would require a rezoning to create a financially feasible project. A rezoning and new development could enhance the aesthetics of the area, help recover the gap in the costs of acquisition between the current value of the utility and the previous owner's selling price, possibly fund innovations related to the CHDL plant, and also provide more residential and office space. More office space is viewed by many as a critical need in the downtown core, as identified by the City's Metro Core Jobs & Economy Land Use Plan, which expressed concern that the office space in the downtown core has been increasingly supplanted by residential towers since residential developments provide developers a much higher rate of return.

In order to formulate redevelopment possibilities for the CHDL plant site, Creative Energy hired the partnership of BIG from Copenhagen and Henriquez Partners Architects. The relatively small site would need to interface with and incorporate an existing utility while being hemmed in by major thoroughfares, and a tall, imposing stadium neighbor. The property is bounded by Beatty Street, the Georgia

Viaduct, and Expo Boulevard. On the other side of Expo Boulevard is BC Place, a sporting arena, which currently serves as home for the BC Lions (Canadian Football League) and the Vancouver Whitecaps FC (Major League Soccer). Completed in 1983, BC Place was constructed in preparation for the World's Fair 1986 (Expo 86) held in Vancouver, and it also served as the site of the opening and closing ceremonies for the 2010 Winter Olympics (XXI Winter Olympic Games). Rogers Arena, home of the Vancouver Canucks (National Hockey League), is situated on the other side of the Georgia Viaduct. In spite of the challenges, there is potential for development and the Creative Energy team has designed solutions where office and residential towers could be placed on the site while incorporating the plant. Any such development would require a rezoning application to be filed and approved.

In addition to the plans for the CHDL plant and its site, Creative Energy has other ideas on how to extend district energy through new creative technologies. The City of Vancouver has an existing extensive Dedicated Fire Protection System that can be used to suppress fires, and would be of critical importance if a major seismic event were to happen in Vancouver. The Dedicated Fire Protection System is a network of dedicated water mains, intake structures, and pump stations that provides ready access to water as part of Vancouver's emergency preparedness plan. Creative Energy believes that the Dedicated Fire Protection System could be converted into a dual-purpose ambient loop. This ambient loop would still be used for fire suppression, but could also provide a way to capture low-grade heat from waste heat from the downtown core and the CHDL plant, as well as sewer heat and ocean heat recovery systems.

Creative Energy has had preliminary discussions with the City about the possibility of piloting this concept in one of Westbank's future developments. (One potential location is its new mixed-use, LEED-platinum development in South Downtown at 1400 Howe Street (adjacent to the north end of the Granville Bridge). The 1400 Howe Development would serve as the centre for the proposed new hot water system for South Downtown and link with the CHDL plant. Even more importantly, it could allow Creative Energy and the City to use the development as a pilot run for converting the Downtown Fire Protection System into a closed-loop ambient temperature system. A pilot could reveal whether current technical and economic assumptions are accurate and how feasible it would be to expand this ambient loop throughout the existing Downtown Fire Protection System. Such a system could radically alter the district energy landscape of downtown Vancouver with tremendous environmental benefits. The discussions between Westbank and the City of Vancouver are still nascent and the ambient loop at this point is still theoretical.

Some might question why a real estate developer would want to purchase a utility in a city where, by law, the returns are capped at nine percent and increased efficiencies are translated into better rates for consumers and a more sustainable future. Ian Gillespie, the sole director of Creative Energy (and the president of Westbank) comes from a family of environmentalists. This is not his first foray into experimenting with energy innovation for his projects. For example, Westbank's TELUS Garden, a one-million-square-foot office, retail, and residential development designed by Henriquez Partners, will feature an efficient and innovative energy system. Within the development there will be a district heating system created in partnership between Westbank and TELUS, and FortisBC will operate a regulated utility within TELUS Garden. The waste heat from the existing TELUS data centre and the new office tower's cooling systems will be recovered to provide heating and hot water for the residential and office towers, as well as for the amenities and retail spaces. These innovations will help the office building become the first LEED Platinum office building in Vancouver. Damon Chan of Westbank said, "TELUS Garden is a mini-version of what we'd like to try to do with the Ambient Loop. You could recover office building heat and transfer it to residential buildings to make downtown much more energy efficient."

Why is a real estate developer interested in energy innovation? It is the goal of city building and innovation and required cooperation by all sectors, including the private sector, to make a more sustainable city. When interviewed by *The Vancouver Sun*'s Kevin Griffin, Ian Gillespie said, "What are cities made up of? Cities are made up of the built environment, they're made up of transportation, they're made up of energy, and they're made up of the social environment . . . . If those are the legs of the stool, how do we get ourselves involved in every piece of that stool? Now that we're a provider of heating to Vancouver, what can we do to remake that system?" Judging from the ambitious vision of Creative Energy's leader, they plan on shaping the future of how energy is generated and delivered throughout downtown Vancouver.

As of March 20, 2016 we chose to relinquish our role in the Creative Energy Project. It was a difficult but necessary decision to keep our boutique studio from growing beyond 60 staff to ensure quality and culture remain uncompromised.

Possible Fuel Switch at the CHDL Plant

Creative Energy plans to explore the possibility of a fuel switch at the CHDL plant. The current plant uses natural gas, a fossil fuel that is still considered in many parts of the world to be a fairly clean source of energy compared to higher carbon options like coal-fired plants. However, the fuel switch would introduce other technologies to reduce the percentage of the plant's load generated by natural gas, which would reduce greenhouse gas emissions. Creative Energy has launched a two-year study, with the support of the City of Vancouver, which is funding 10 percent of the study. The fuel switch study would examine the kinds of renewable energy sources and technologies that could be used at the CHDL plant, the timeline for implementation, and what they would cost.

Possible fuel switch solutions include more renewable energy sources like sewer heat recovery, geoexchange (taking heat from water or the ground with a pump), biomass (the use of biological materials like wood waste or biofuels), or waste-conversion systems (using new technologies to produce energy from garbage or other waste streams). The study focuses on how implementing a fuel switch, with the resultant reductions in greenhouse gases, could help the City achieve its 2020 goal and assist in securing Vancouver's sustainable future. In addition to the environmental benefits, the conversion of the distribution process, the development of the land, and the fuel switch would all be a source of jobs for the city. Also, localized energy systems need to become more robust as part of cities' strategies to build more resilient energy systems, especially in the wake of natural disasters and grid shutdowns as seen recently on the east coast of the United States after Hurricane Sandy in October 2012, and in Toronto after a major ice storm in December 2013.

VANCOUVER NORM

RETAIL

60 W CORDOVA

RETAIL

An Affordable Home Ownership Experiment
60 West Cordova Street

"…silhouettes of people standing on each other's shoulders, helping each other, holding up the building. We think it is a beautiful metaphor for the building."

GREGORY HENRIQUEZ

MOST PEOPLE AGREE: one of the biggest crises facing Vancouver is one of affordability. How do you keep the urban centre diverse and vibrant with people of all backgrounds, occupations, and economic levels when the cost of living is increasingly out of reach for many people? How do you prevent the brain drain of the younger generation when even young professionals perceive that they cannot afford to live in Vancouver and raise their families here without a struggle? One of the traditional keys to achieving stability and accumulating wealth is to own property, but with the average two-storey house in metro Vancouver consuming approximately 80 percent of the average household income, how can that be achievable?

This struggle for affordability in Vancouver, particularly with respect to home ownership, inspired the affordable home ownership project of 60 West Cordova. Within days of commencing sales, even with consciously minimal marketing to keep project costs low, the 96 units at 60 West Cordova sold out. From a sales perspective, Vancouver's first affordable ownership experiment was a success.

In an effort to create a community within the building that had an existing connection to the neighbourhood, the purchasers had to prove

← **60 WEST CORDOVA**
In Gastown, just east of
Abbott Street and the
Woodward's Development.

that they currently worked, lived, or volunteered in the Downtown Eastside, including Gastown or Chinatown. The development partners, Westbank and Vancity, also made an explicit decision to keep the units affordable. In this case, affordability meant that at least 50 percent of the market-rate units were priced such that buyers with an income of less than $36,500 could qualify for a mortgage based on Vancity's underwriting.

The pricing structure allowed the purchase of units by moderate-income people who had previously believed that they were shut out of home ownership in central Vancouver. The media coverage at the time featured some of the people who purchased units expressing their surprise at achieving something they hadn't even dreamed was within their reach. "I never thought I'd be able to buy in Vancouver," Gillian Ryckman told *The Vancouver Sun*. Ryckman, a young nurse at St. Paul's Hospital who volunteered in the Downtown Eastside, was able to purchase one of the units at 60 West Cordova.

Another buyer, John Jones, was training to be a bookkeeper at Glasshouse, a charitable organization that provides operational support to other charities. Jones has Asperger's Syndrome, and stability and routine are even more important for him than for the average person. His mother, Sharon Wilkie, told *The Vancouver Sun*, "People with Asperger's have difficulty with changes. He needs to be in a stable environment hopefully for years or the rest of his life. So getting him into a place where he doesn't have to move and is close to work—it will mean a great deal to his life." In a news clip on Global TV, Wilkie looked visibly relieved that her son was able to buy one of these units, "We're just thrilled. It sets my mind at ease because as a mother I want to make sure that John is taken care of and he has his place in this world when I am gone."

The demand for the 96 units exceeded the development partners' expectations. This was a largely unexplored market and there were decisions made to keep to keep the units affordable, with smaller units, modest finishes, and extremely limited parking keeping costs down. There was a prerequisite for a community tie with the Downtown Eastside and a requirement that the buyers live in the unit and not resell for at least a year. The hope was that a resale provision would deter buyers who were not planning on living in the home long term, and would allow people who were strongly invested in the existing community to be able to own in that neighbourhood. All of these factors meant that the developers believed the units would sell, but until they did sell, it was an untested market. The developers were taking a calculated risk in an experiment that succeeded. The sales response suggests that a stronger restriction on resale could be supported, and this would further lower prices by discouraging speculative buying. It would also increase owner-occupation, and build a stronger sense of community in the buildings.

In addition to the affordable market units, there are 12 non-market ownership units. These units were sold at cost to the PHS Community Services Society (PHS) and Habitat for Humanity of Greater Vancouver (Habitat for Humanity) to enable them to sell these units at below-market rates to people meeting the requirements of their respective programs.

PHS is a non-profit development organization with a long history

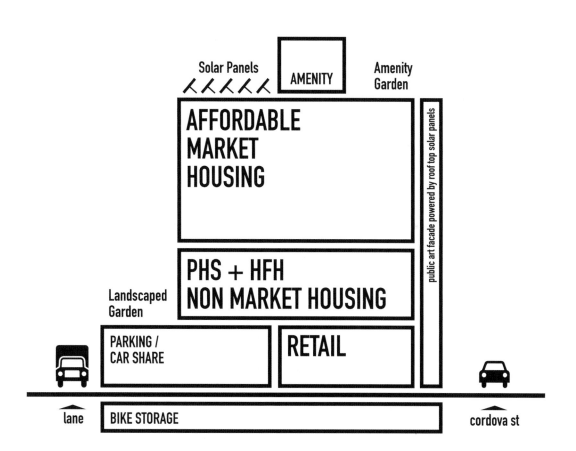

Solar Panels

AMENITY

Amenity
Garden

AFFORDABLE
MARKET
HOUSING

public art facade powered by roof top solar panels

PHS + HFH
NON MARKET HOUSING

Landscaped
Garden

PARKING /
CAR SHARE

RETAIL

lane

BIKE STORAGE

cordova st

PROGRAM DIAGRAM

serving the lower-income residents of the Downtown Eastside. Their focus is on affordable, supportive housing and services needed by the lower-income community such as medical and dental care, and banking. PHS serves those who are often not served well by society—the homeless or those at risk of homelessness, and people who are often faced with other severe challenges like mental illness or drug addiction. Along with Vancouver Coastal Health, they also run the only safe-injection site in North America. With their long-standing commitment to the community, they were a natural choice to receive eight units from the developer at cost in order to provide long-term workers of PHS (or other non-profit organizations serving the needs of the Downtown Eastside population) a chance to own in the neighbourhood where they work and often already lived. One happy resident who purchased a unit held by PHS is a man who had worked for decades at another not-for-profit doing work-training programs for at-risk youth.

Habitat for Humanity is a non-profit that mobilizes volunteers and community partners to build affordable housing for lower-income adults and families. Homes are made affordable by being sold without requirement of a down paymen and financed with no interest mortgages. People becoming homeowners through the program are also required to invest "sweat equity" (500 hours of their own labour) constructing homes and supporting the organization. 60 West Cordova enabled four condominiums (one- and two-bedroom units) to become homes for Habitat for Humanity participants.

60 West Cordova was an attempt to create a prototype of affordable ownership that could succeed in Vancouver and expand home ownership to people of moderate income. So how did this affordable ownership experiment happen? In 2009, Vancity foreclosed on a mortgage it held on a parking lot on West Cordova near Abbott Street. The

lot had been purchased by developer Robert Wilson in 2007 for $7.9 million. With the repossession, Vancity became the owner of the lot (situated on the cusp of Gastown and the Downtown Eastside), which was then valued at $2.5 million less than what the developer paid for it in 2007. Vancity had two options: they could sell the lot to a developer, or they could try to develop it. Justin Stubbs of Vancity was a champion for the idea that, with the right development partner, Vancity could get its money back out of the property, maybe even make a profit, and see something developed consistent with its community-based values. Vancity entered discussions with Ian Gillespie of Westbank on possibly partnering to develop this property.

Westbank had recently responded to a public solicitation for redevelopment plans for an approximately 15-acre development called Little Mountain. Little Mountain was constructed in 1954 as a social housing community within the broader Riley Park neighbourhood located to the east of Queen Elizabeth Park. In 2007, it went from federal ownership to provincial control. The province, led by BC Housing, then entered into an agreement with the City of Vancouver for the redevelopment of Little Mountain. Westbank put together a team, including the Peterson Group and Henriquez Partners Architects, and developed an innovative proposal containing retail and a varied mix of housing types. These included standard-market housing, compact market housing (smaller units with optional parking to keep costs low), competitive-market housing (where units would be discounted 25 percent to help enable affordability and BC Housing would receive an ongoing 25 percent endowment in exchange for the discounted property), and non-market housing for BC Housing's provincial social housing programs.

Even though another developer was ultimately the successful bidder on the Little Mountain project, the ideas generated by the

Westbank team in their proposal about a mix of housing types were conceptual seeds planted for that team. Gillespie was excited about the possibility of a development that might result in an affordable ownership component. When he entered into discussions with Vancity, this idea was at the forefront of his mind. Gillespie's idea was that if one could somehow limit the speculative value of real estate as a commodity by requiring people to live in the place they purchased, one could inherently limit its value and render it affordable to a greater number of people. He also really wanted to try an affordable housing experiment in a context free of government subsidy. As Gillespie explained, "In the old days, the way you got affordable housing done was one of the three levels of government—often more than one level—made contributions to make housing happen and that is how it has worked in western democracies since World War II. As the costs of health care have completely undermined the ability of the [federal] government to do anything other than health care, housing has really suffered. So we were wondering, how can we be part of the solution?"

This housing experiment would require a developer willing to take some financial risk and lower returns on investment than its typical market returns. Vancity would need to be willing to contribute the land into the deal and utilize its flexible, innovative mortgage financing for people who might be able to afford the monthly mortgage payment but are not able to come up with the standard down payment required.

Westbank brought in Henriquez Partners, and in turn, they solicited the involvement of PHS. All three had worked together closely on the Woodward's Redevelopment, so it was a natural team. A City of Vancouver staffer suggested that Habitat for Humanity would be an appropriate addition to the project and the team agreed. The collaborators were now in place. It would require some assistance from the City with respect to zoning, but this project—the first of its kind in Vancouver—would be entirely privately funded. The innovative structure and risk involved for this affordable-home-ownership project was a pilot of a new private, socially conscious development model.

While the City of Vancouver did not fund the project, the City still had a necessary role in helping the project succeed. First of all, the project was done within existing zoning, but the City had the authority to allow the project to be one hundred feet high instead of 75, which they permitted as well as agreeing to a minimal level of parking that did not meet the parking bylaw for the City. The limited number of parking stalls—18 stalls, two of which were allocated for car-share programs—did several important things for the project. It made it attractive to buyers who lived and worked in the area because they did not need a car on a daily basis, it encouraged a reduction in car use yielding environmental benefits, and, most crucially, each parking stall not built helped lower the cost of each unit by $40,000-$50,000. This was an important component in enabling the developer to offer affordable unit prices.

The City of Vancouver also required agreements legally restricting and protecting the purpose of the 12 units sold at cost to PHS and Habitat for Humanity. Because of the novelty of these below-market home ownership units being conveyed to non-profits in Vancouver, the City needed assistance in drafting the Housing Agreement so they brought in a consultant: Tim Wake, the former Housing Administrator for the Whistler Housing Authority. While at the Whistler Housing Authority, Wake worked on many of these types of housing arrangements, which were required to create an affordable housing supply for the civil servants and workers needed to run and support an expensive resort town.

For Metro Vancouver, Gregory Henriquez thinks that this afford-able housing experiment has the potential to be a very successful model. "There is a depth to this market that remains untapped. If someone wants to do this, it is a fabulous model," he says. Gillespie agrees, "We could have sold this [project] four or five times over. The demand was insatiable." Henriquez believes that government is appro-priately focussing their resources on higher priority housing needs, for example, housing the homeless, seniors, and families. However, for a private development community willing to think more broadly, there are many moderate-income people who want to achieve the dream of home ownership and are willing to live with smaller units with no parking and modest finishes. The price of real estate in Vancouver makes it prohibitively expensive for low-to-moderate income people to own their own home or condominium, particularly downtown or close to the downtown core. Many people in this income bracket choose to purchase farther away from their jobs or opt to rent, particu-larly since Vancouver has such a large discrepancy between the costs of a mortgage versus renting a comparable space. One outcome of this pilot project is that, prior to this affordable home ownership experi-ment it was rare to see "affordable ownership" described as a part of the housing continuum in Vancouver. However, as concerns of affordabil-ity increase and experiments like this one have taken place, affordable ownership has become more frequently represented as part of the housing continuum, and has become a greater part of the dialogue around housing concerns in the city.

Could this model be replicated to help more Vancouverites achieve home ownership? It seems clear that the same partners, with the ben-efit of the learning from this project, or similarly-minded organizations, could replicate this model in other Vancouver neighbourhoods,

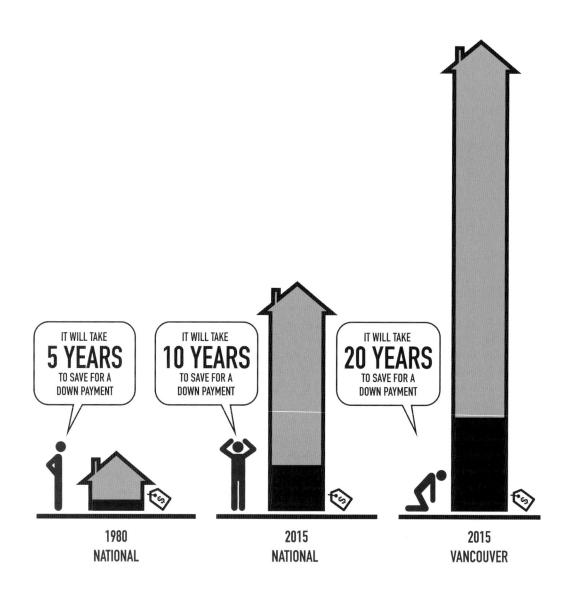

IT WILL TAKE
5 YEARS
TO SAVE FOR A
DOWN PAYMENT

IT WILL TAKE
10 YEARS
TO SAVE FOR A
DOWN PAYMENT

IT WILL TAKE
20 YEARS
TO SAVE FOR A
DOWN PAYMENT

1980
NATIONAL

2015
NATIONAL

2015
VANCOUVER

HOUSING PRICE

20% DOWN PAYMENT

especially those walkable to people's jobs or close to transit. It also proves that, for committed developers and innovative, socially conscious lenders like Vancity, these affordable ownership units could succeed as part of a larger market-rate development project. The financial models of larger projects can provide more flexibility in supporting a mix of housing types including affordable ownership.

This project was a success largely because of the relationships involved in its development, as the metaphor of the public art on its façade suggests. The façade is silk-screened silhouettes of people standing on each other's shoulders as if helping each other, and holding up the building. Finally, the 60 West Cordova project relied on collaboration by an enlightened real estate developer willing to take risks on a socially conscious project, a local financing institution with resources and a mission of community investment and innovation to meet challenging needs, the flexibility of the City of Vancouver in zoning to allow for experimentation, and non-profit organizations, including one with a deep history and relationship with the community it has served for decades. In 2014, the project won a Special Jury Award at the Vancouver Urban Design Awards for "reinforcing community through collaboration and social innovation." Hopefully the 60 West Cordova project can serve as a prototype for affordable home ownership in Vancouver. Whether or not this model is replicable and transportable to other North American cities will be explored in the conclusion of this book.

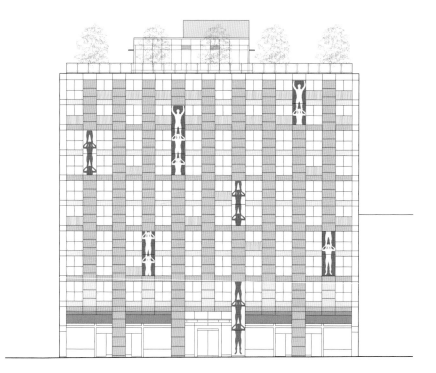

60 WEST CORDOVA
NORTH ELEVATION

0   2   5   10   15   25

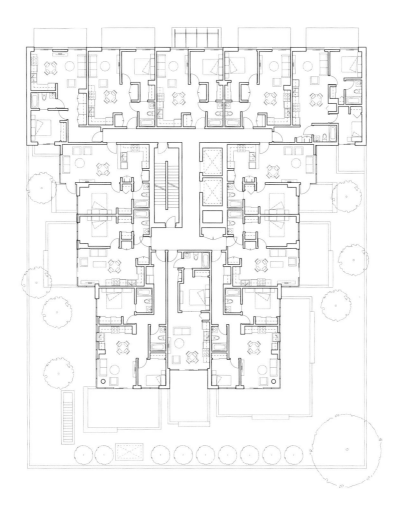

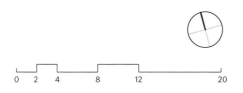

0 2 4   8   12   20

60 WEST CORDOVA
FLOOR PLAN LEVEL 2

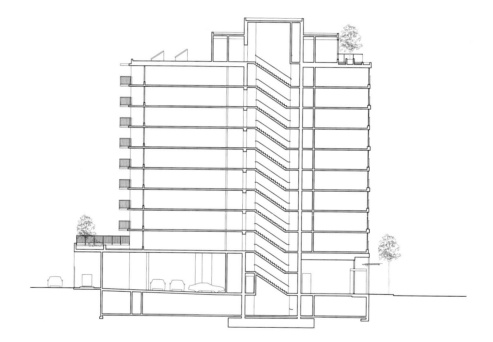

60 WEST CORDOVA
SECTION

0   2   5   10   15   25

Conclusion

MARYA COTTEN GOULD

The Future of the Citizen City

A CITIZEN CITY is a vibrant, culturally rich city where people from disparate backgrounds and economic levels are included in the urban community. In many ways, Vancouver comes close to achieving this ideal. Largely the values held by those who live here support this vision. The City leadership is concerned about affordable housing, homelessness, and sustainability of the community. The general ethos of Canadians is consistent with a belief in an inclusive community regardless of background or country of origin, and that economic disparity should not be so severe that there are citizens who are homeless or do not enjoy a basic standard of health and welfare in a comparatively rich and stable country.

However, Vancouver still has progress to make and cannot rest on its laurels and current international acclaim with respect to its urban planning and liveability. The values are present that make it possible for Vancouver to achieve Citizen City status, but the challenges facing the city are profound and will require the deployment of all sectors to make greater strides towards its achievement becoming a reality. The cost of real estate and high cost of living in comparison to average incomes means that homelessness and the lack of affordable housing are intractable problems. All levels of government need to focus on the need to have shelter for all Canadians. This is incredibly important, particularly at a time when Canada is moving forward with a new prime minister after a long period of the national government having abandoned housing as one of its priorities. For example, over the last 25 years there has been a 46 percent decrease in federal spending for affordable housing (Levitz). Promoting sustainability and protecting liveability means people should be able to afford to live where they work and not travel great distances in their daily commute. The city needs to attract and retain industries and a range of employment opportunities so working people have a chance at home ownership and the stability and wealth-building it brings. Wealth should not just arrive from offshore.

Integration of the newest Canadians into the city and establishing a cohesive sense of identity while honouring diversity continues to be a challenging situation. Changing demographics and the increased need for density due to growth and sustainability concerns means that the city landscape is changing. This change provokes an array of emotional responses from people with differing appetites for change. Achieving enough cultural cohesion to create an overall sense of city community will be difficult, but not impossible, if projects continue to be developed that encourage diversity within neighbourhoods and promote inclusion instead of greater segregation by race, immigration status, or economic class.

Creative partnerships in real estate development are an important step towards meeting these needs within a city, and towards becoming a Citizen City. Innovative cross-sector partnerships can help house the homeless, create more affordable housing, promote culture, improve infrastructure, and protect the most vulnerable. The case studies here showcase well-intentioned, novel projects or proposals that are an effort towards making Vancouver a Citizen City. The projects (or project proposals) had varying degrees of success. Examining which projects were the most successful (and why) can help elucidate best practices for these kinds of cooperative development ventures.

The Woodward's Redevelopment was successful because it involved all three levels of government, longstanding non-profit organizations that had the trust of the community, and a motivated development team. The mobilization of all the parties was a combination of hard work and dedication and timely political will. The Woodward's Redevelopment symbolizes the necessity of getting buy in by all necessary parties, prioritizing community inclusion, and the progress that can be made when private motivation and political will are present at the same time. (The redevelopment of this site had been attempted many times before. It is also a lesson in civic perseverance.)

The success of the Woodward's Redevelopment and its values-driven approach, as well as the lessons learned along the way, spawned the so-called "Children of Woodward's" projects described in the preceeding case studies. These projects also reflect the importance of galvanizing political will and community support at a fortuitous time. The former remand centre housing project, the York Theatre revitalization, the 6th & Fir condominium building, and the new refugee Welcome House Centre are all examples of the motivation of private actors matching up with political support. Timing plays a crucial role here as well. All four of these projects had been contemplated in some form for a long time (in some cases, decades) but needed the staunch motivation of the current project parties to push them through to completion.

Another element that breeds success in achieving a Citizen City is bold experimentation. The affordable condominium units of 60 West Cordova sold out in a matter of days, and proved it could be a workable model for other affordable ownership projects. The centralized services-delivery model of the refugee Welcome House Centre and the mixed-use project by the Central Presbyterian Church are both unique models that, when built, could prove to be workable approaches for other future projects. The proposed infrastructure experimentation and greening by Creative Energy evidences how a developer can engage at a greater level in city-building.

The greatest challenges faced in these projects (or proposed projects) were the perennial lack of government or non-profit funding, the political realities (including conflicts even among like-minded advocates for the same community), and people and communities who were entrenched in their viewpoints, resistant to change, or focussed on their own self-interest.

Can the successful projects described in this book be replicated across North America and beyond, or is this a uniquely Vancouver story? Motivated and progressive cities throughout North America can be poised to create policies to encourage the kind of projects that are featured in this book. However, there are factors that make Vancouver a particularly fertile environment for these kinds of cooperative development partnerships. As stated previously, Canadians embrace a basic standard of living for all citizens as a fundamental right more heartily than their neighbours to the south. (For example, Canadians have embraced the idea that all people deserve a certain level of health care, which is still a very controversial issue in the United States.) This difference in ideology is also apparent in the treatment of homeless people. Most Canadians believe the homeless deserve to have a basic home (even if the political reality means that with finite resources there is not always the government funding available that there should be to make this possible).

Canada's "mosaic" metaphor (instead of a "melting pot") is symbolic of a more positive view of diversity than in the United States. Canadian political discourse regarding immigration does not generally suffer from the same vitriol that runs rampant in the American political discourse. (Although it is true that the United States grapples with the problem of illegal immigration to a much greater extent than Canada does.) Even within the Canadian context, Vancouver may be unique in its broader sense of social and economic inclusion relative to other cities. (A simple example is that mixed-income projects in Toronto often have separate entrances in the building for the different levels of housing. In Vancouver it is much more likely that everyone will use the same entrances and elevators.)

Vancouver's success in innovative cross-sector projects is due in part to the City's zoning and urban planning policies that encourage city amenities being funded by value extracted from the development process, primarily via the Community Amenity Contribution. Vancouver is known for its emphasis on urban planning and its progressive ideas with respect to city-building. The emphasis on high-quality urban planning and a zoning system that allows for some discretion means that Vancouver can serve as an urban laboratory in a way that other cities may not be able to without restructuring their development policies or allocating additional resources.

Additionally, the size of Vancouver means that the players in the development, government, and non-profit arenas tend to know each other. There are "repeat players," which means that interactions require a higher level of accountability and professionalism, because one will interact with people in these organizations over and over again—these are typically not one-time interactions. Like any industry that requires political approval, the development process can become very personal.

Organizations are comprised of individuals, each with a performance history, motivations, and personalities. (In a relatively small city with discretion in its zoning system, flexibility in favour of a developer can be perceived as favoritism for a particular developer or a victory for the wealthy and powerful. This is a common critique. Proponents of the system argue that the favourable results are the result of laudable past and present performances by the development teams and the value extractions by the City which can benefit the community.) In a best-case scenario, progress is made when there is an alignment of values among the developers shaping the city, the people who live in the city, and those in government.

In any transaction that relies on cooperation among organizations, especially those from different sectors with different motivations, relationships are critical. Throughout all of these projects a critical factor in getting an idea or design to a physical reality is relationships among the parties. While hard to quantify, the existence of good working relationships and a basis of trust among the parties served as a foundation for these projects, which enabled progress when the projects might have otherwise stalled. These relationships are of utmost importance for any project, but are particularly salient in Vancouver, where the size of the city both forges the relationships and makes them critical for success. For the architect, the value-add to the development process goes beyond design prowess. It is also about business acumen and credibility brought to the process due to relationships. The stop-gap housing proposal, the former remand centre housing project, and the passarelle were all architect-driven ideas. In the development process for the ISS of BC's Welcome House Centre and the redevelopment by the Central Presbyterian Church, Gregory Henriquez played a key role in assembling the development team. A high level of trust due to past transactions can add gravitas to an architect's role. This is a powerful reason that the modern, ethical architect should focus not only on winning design awards, but should be an engaged citizen and active in the civic affairs of the community where they work. Architects should be architects not just of buildings, but also of their vision for a vibrant, inclusive Citizen City. Civic engagement by the design community is critical in pursuing the vision of a Citizen City.

Civic engagement should not be limited to the design community. There are roles for all members of the community to play in a Citizen City. All denizens of a Citizen City should feel empowered to be engaged in their city by whatever means they see fit: contributing ideas, joining organizations, challenging the government, running for public office, starting a blog, championing a project, and taking any action they can in making cities as vibrant and inclusive as humanly possible.

Afterword

AN INTERVIEW WITH GREGORY HENRIQUEZ
BY ROBERT ENRIGHT

Letter to the Young Architect

ROBERT ENRIGHT: It took you a long enough time to complete the Woodward's project that while the metaphor of being knocked off your horse on the road to an Eastside Damascus may not be entirely apt, I do get a sense that Woodward's was a kind of epiphany.

GREGORY HENRIQUEZ: You're right. Prior to Woodward's, I saw developers as the type of people I didn't want to have lunch with, let alone work with. The profane world of making money was something I didn't want to be a part of. Even though my father and I had worked episodically as mini-developers ourselves, and we understood what they did, somehow I couldn't marry their values with meaningful architecture. I regarded my social housing and community centres as projects that had to be independent of that profane world because I believed they were connected to larger and more important societal issues. What I didn't understand was the power of the development process to do good in the world if properly harnessed. Through Woodward's I realized that if you have an enlightened civic government; if you have a developer who is willing to do good in exchange for appropriate financial compensation; if you have a community willing to engage in that dialogue; and if you have a project of substance that could actually benefit from these relationships, then something meaningful may happen. Woodward's was one of those rare circumstances where three levels of government came together and where a community united because it realized there was a crisis that had to be dealt with. The City was smart enough to pick a developer willing to do the right thing and the developer was smart enough to see it as an opportunity too so that not only could making money be seen as something of value, but contributing back to the larger community could also be an integral part of the development goals. I think the whole history of the City of Vancouver's Community Amenity Contributions was evolving over many years under the leadership of Larry Beasley and many city councils, and it crystallized in Woodward's. So there was an epiphany, which sounds trite, but what occurred to me was that if all levels of government and the community worked together, a lot could be accomplished.

Is it the scale of the project that allowed all those 'ifs' to find a way to work together? Could a smaller project have brought the same realization?
That's a good question. Possibly. I think the shift occurred because for the first time you had a city council that wanted to play an active role in changing the paradigm. Larry Campbell was a newly elected mayor; you had Jim Green, a social activist; you had a left-leaning party willing to make the deals necessary to control what they thought was a very important piece of land, and they wanted to listen to the community. The projects I've done since —we call them the 'Children of Woodward's'—build upon the lessons I learned from Woodward's. But the larger scale of the project made it especially poignant. We took an entire block of the historic centre of the city that was boarded up and surrounded by drug dealers, where there was an HIV epidemic being addressed by the Portland Hotel Society with the safe injection site, and we helped change it for the better. You can argue as to whether it was too successful, and whether there was too much gentrification, but we did it and it was done through a collective civic effort. It couldn't have happened without Ian Gillespie and Ben Yeung, the two

developers who were willing to take on the financial risk. As I say, when ingenuity in the private sector is partnered with the goals and aspirations of a community, and when there is the political will to stay on the right rails, then things can really happen for the better.

But you can have ingenuity in a private sector that isn't prepared to give away its profit. So it obviously takes a certain kind of entrepreneurial ingenuity to agree to certain social ideas.

Exactly. Generally speaking, developers measure their success by profit margins and it's only later in life that they start collecting art or giving back to society. They reflect upon what they've done and ask if it is meaningful enough only to have made money. Apparently a very high percentage of computer programmers have "found God" and the explanation some of them provide is that, because their work is devoid of spirituality, they need to look for it elsewhere. I think the same thing is true with developers— many of them have things in their lives that compensate for the lack of spiritual, artistic, or creative dimension in what they do. Ian Gillespie is a rare developer in the sense that he sees a project as a complete work of art and has a whole series of strategies to integrate his aesthetic and environmental vision. He has even used Bauhaus terms to articulate that idea.

Prior to Woodward's you had talked about what architecture could do in society in ethical terms. It came from a combination of example and education. Was that ethic a useful thing to carry forward into the Woodward's project?

Yes. One of the things my father taught me is that you always have to speak the truth, whatever your truth is. People can tell the difference between authentic and inauthentic communication. We all know when we're sitting beside someone who actually cares versus someone who is pretending to care. I have come to understand through consultation processes that if you authentically listen, people will cut you a lot of slack. They will see your intentions are good and they'll work with you to make the project achieve its full potential.

Were there more stakeholders involved in the Woodward's project than in anything you had worked on before?
It's probably the most complex mixed-use project in the history of Canada, with more diverse stakeholders; the homeless community and residents in the neighbourhood, the university, the federal government, the City, as well as two non-profit housing providers. With so many voices, someone was required to be the hinge, or the interpreter of the diverse languages of this babble. Someone had to put the collective voices into a form that could make sense of the whole and within which everyone could live. That someone was the architect.

Babble is an interesting term, because a babble has to be translated into a language understandable to all the people speaking through the project.
We were going so fast we had to let all the languages be what they were and we piled one language on top of another. My father would say, 'There are too many things going on. We're not going to be able to do all these things in one project. We'll have to put some across the street.' I had thought it would be a self-selecting process, in that certain things would get eliminated because the funding wouldn't materialize, or someone would get cold feet, but everyone stayed in. So we ended up with a bizarre hybrid. You have a building with a food store, the NFB office, social and market housing, the Attorney General, a tiny smoke shop, a dentist, and a sushi restaurant. And that's only one of the buildings. What is beautiful is that it

mirrors more eclectic European or even Asian cities, where zoning isn't legislated, where everything can mutually coexist. It happened by chance and could not be repeated today in Vancouver.

One of Vancouver's advantages is that it has a fairly flexible zoning system where things can actually be negotiated. Nobody brings a set of the 10 Urban Commandments down from the mountaintop?
Vancouver has a history of what's called Spot Re-zoning, Comprehensive Districts, or CD1s. That's what we do at HPA. All our projects are site-specific zoning, so we re-zone every site to a specific use based upon what our client, the community, and the city agree is the most meaningful thing to happen. The Vancouver planning process is set up to do just this. There had been so many attempts to save Woodward's, the site, and the neighbourhood, and they had all failed, so everyone wanted to believe it was possible given this new paradigm of collaboration and change of leadership. For some reason, everyone trusted us. I'll never forget going to Cameron Gray, the director of The Housing Centre for the city and saying we had 200 units of social housing. I asked what percentage should be SRO (Single Room Occupancy) replacement and what percentage should be family housing and he said, 'I don't know, you tell me. What works on the site?' Every decision, and there were myriad, was like that.

Are you a patient man? It seems to me that there must have been moments when you wanted to scream with frustration.
I wasn't in a reflective frame of mind at the time. We were problem-solving every day— there was a whole team of people led by Peter Wood, one of our Directors of Architecture, working on aesthetic issues, zoning issues, and on community and programming issues. We had financial parameters and we had to go fast.

Alberto Pérez-Gómez, with whom you studied, says that for an architect to take a leading role in society, he or she has to have a number of skills: "the architect must be a social activist, a realist, a poet, a political technician and a utopian." The list itself may be utopian. Does that person exist in the profession?

I don't think one person can play all the required roles. What I believe he meant was that these are a myriad of issues we have to wrestle with in order to be effective in today's society. We all aspire to be those things, and each project requires different ingredients. But he is right, you need a bit of each skill set, and in ideal circumstances you'd have a diverse team of people to make it happen. I grew up in the profession, so I have a bit of a head start on the role of the architect in society. My father did social housing. He is a great architect and he is a great role model, not only in terms of his ethics and his aesthetic drive, but in his overall commitment to society. He trained me from early childhood to be an architect, so I owe him a huge debt. What Alberto taught me was the historical context and how the role of the architect has shifted to being a problem-solver or a branded form-giver, which is very useful for marketing, and that there needs to be a more profound engagement in society for our role to become meaningful again. That's where the activist and the utopian parts come in. Of course, you have to be a realist, and you have to be a technician, and ideally, you have to be poet, and we have tried to nurture all these within our practice. The marriage of civic activism, design dexterity, and understanding the nature of the development process allows us to participate fully in the creation stage of a project.

I would have thought the one necessary thing in this whole process is to be a realist. This book says that, "expectations need to be tempered as optimism and passion meet with realism," and so the crunch comes when all that passion comes face-to-face with what is realistic.

My dad always used to say to me when I was little, that 'you have to dream the possible dream.' It still has to be a dream and it has to be a new reality, but it has to be a possible one. And it has to have a reason for being as well, otherwise you are setting yourself up for theoretical investigations, which are utopian and remain on paper. Theoretical architectural explorations are important, too, and future generations can learn from them. There are a number of famous architects who haven't built anything and have still contributed in a meaningful way. Our practice, though, has been about actually executing buildings.

I was trying to figure out what Alberto meant by 'political technician' and I get a sense he is saying you have to understand the political terrain in which you're operating.

There are three parts to that component. You have to understand policy, that there is inertia within the bureaucracy, and just as important, you have to understand the relationships among people who have power and how they relate to one another at any given time. There are all sorts of variations—the bureaucracy can be very strong and the politicians can be weak, or the reverse can be the case. So appreciating how things ebb and flow in relation to individuals is a very important piece of any successful business or, for that matter, of any endeavour in life. You don't get that training in art school or in architectural school, where what is being espoused is purely aesthetic or conceptual.

The critic and editor, Meeka Walsh, sees bureaucracy in Kafkaesque terms. It aims for self-perpetuation; it is about inertia and putting impediments in the way of things getting done. I gather your sense of how bureaucracies operate is not nearly so bleak?

There's no question that she is right. But the key is to recognize the intentions of the policy and to get beneath the surface of its rules and regulations. If you can find a way to understand the intentions, and if they are good, then there's often a way to work around perceived limitations. But it requires an open dialogue with individuals who are willing come up with a solution that represents the spirit of those intentions. I'm in a project right now where we're arguing about process in terms of disclosure to the public. We know the end product is going to provide more and larger family units for the community, which is something the city wants, but we've already shown the public something else. So the question is, do we have to go back to the public or not? How do you navigate through this question? There are countless things like that on each project, and so the stamina required to make sure that each one of them happens, while also addressing any poetic aspirations, requires a focus and a commitment that most architects are not up for.

And it requires some pretty fancy dancing. I can think of two of your projects—the York Theatre Revitalization for one—where the bureaucracy was basically overruled by City Council, and where you argued the Bridgeport Guidelines had to be re-interpreted. One of your strategies in dealing with bureaucracy is to try and reframe what it is they're doing.
It also depends on the context of the specific time and place. When Council overruled the recommendation of their own Planning Department, it was Gregor Robertson's and Vision's first Council meeting. They were very idealistic and our group capitalized on it. But they might not so easily approve the York Theatre arrangement today; they would understand the real concern the bureaucracy had and they would recognize that they may be setting a dangerous funding precedent. I've tried to use 100 percent amenity density to fund similar civic-oriented projects again and again, and I've not been successful. We are constantly pushing the limits and

experimenting with new funding models in our practice—we challenge everything, and people sometimes get frustrated with us in the Planning Department. They say, 'Why can't you just do what's in the zoning? We wrote the zoning for a reason,' and I'll say, 'Well, it doesn't seem to be the right solution and I have a client who wants to do something better and we have aspirations to contribute bigger and you wrote this compromised community plan and you are aware there are all sorts of problems.' So we get into these Kafkaesque dialogues on a daily basis. But to go back to an earlier point in the conversation, as long as you are speaking your truth and are honestly trying to do something better for society, then no one can fault you for trying.

The poet comes up in Alberto's list and I want to get a sense of how important the poetic dimension is in the overall process of building a better urban environment?

In some projects the poetry emerges organically— it just oozes out of the project's ground. Others you have to work really hard on. Given that each project we take on is unique, the question becomes where is the soft spot that allows you to touch something spiritual, or something larger than just a place to house someone. They're all different. The Honest Ed's Project we're working on in Toronto right now came from a trip I took to Tokyo with my son Jacob, during which I saw these miniature buildings emerging vertically from little storefronts. On Bloor and Bathurst, many people were talking to us about wanting to keep the retail frontage really fine-grained to ensure against big box retailing. So we thought translating the Tokyo model (which was also informed by New York's Union Square) to Bloor and Bathurst might be a workable way of responding to the site. These are lessons learned elsewhere that can be re-interpreted into a poetic strategy for a project in another place and time.

You talk about an integral relationship between ethics and aesthetics and it seems to me that the aesthetic body often gets tailored to fit the ethical bed. Does the aesthetic dimension get short-changed when ethics, or when practical considerations, come along.

For the Greeks, in order for it to be ethical, it had to be beautiful and the reverse was also the case. We have separated the two. Unfortunately, we see a lot of empty formalism. A number of the most famous architects in the world are what I call form-stuffers—they make some form, they twist or extrude something, or chop something up into pieces and collage it together, and then they fit in a program afterwards.

I can't imagine who you're talking about.

It could be Frank Gehry. It could be anyone, right? Some are more minimalist. But they are form-stuffers and they have a style, very much like a fashion designer. When you go to them, you're buying a style and the style can be marketed under the guise of a series of aesthetic or environmental concerns. Sometimes they're artists and that's fine, too. But the problem is those projects look the way they do because the fundamental underpinnings aren't about the local context, nor do they address the meaningful larger issues we must confront as a society. Or even worse, they reflect our hidden values as a culture of consumption. Often, they reflect the values of a culture that wants to consume this aesthetic object for whatever reason, whether for prestige or to make money, to feel better about itself, or to anaesthetize us, rather than to fundamentally aspire to something of more substance. If you have more humanitarian values, there are better things you can do to improve life on this planet than to build another Frank Gehry art gallery. As pretty as they are, I believe it is Disneyland masquerading as culture.

So is there no Henriquez Partners style? Each building is generated out of its own self-defining principles?

I'm not one to judge how it looks in the end. The intention is that it emerges out of an authentic exploration. Obviously, every painter has a brush stroke and so you can't get away from being yourself. That said, the driving force behind the way the project appears—the way it functions and the way it is articulated and comes into being—is out of this exploration of what matters.

And what matters is something embedded in the site or in the city itself? How determining are those things in what you build?

I think that at Bloor and Bathurst, for example, the outcome can be a direct reflection of the values of the community, because the community values are in sync with some very profound aspirations that we share with our developer. They are humanist values: to provide rental housing, a public market, a bike co-op, urban architecture, a daycare, artists' studios, and to create micro retail curated by Tonya Surman of CSI, all of which is local and meaningful to the people in the neighbourhood.

And to sustain and augment the community that is already there.

Yes. We talk about cultural sustainability in our practice. In ideal circumstances, it is easy because we're simply arguing about the expression: should it be this high or that density? These are the local projects we all covet. There are also projects where the community may not be in sync with what we believe to be important. The project at 1401 Comox Street in Vancouver was a case where some of the involved people living directly adjacent to the project didn't believe rental housing was as important as other issues.

Was the surprise in that project that the people who rejected rental housing seemed like traitors to the way they themselves were living?
Yes. The City staff had this unfortunate name for the project, it was called STIR Housing—Short Term Incentives for Rent—so it sounded like we were stirring up problems. Many of us thought it was the most obvious thing in the world. In Vancouver there had been no rental housing built in a generation because condominiums make a lot more money, so there are no incentives to build rental housing. It was 2008, there was a recession, and we had a developer who was willing to convince a church to sell him the land at a reduced price to build rental housing. We were working with people in the neighbourhood and a gay and lesbian community group to do a community centre and I thought, 'How could this not be great?' Instead, we get a petition with 10,000 signatures in support of the West End Plan. So the question was, 'What do you do? Does the community win? Do we build condominiums and give the money to the aquatic centre?' Our client would have made more money doing that but he and our elected City Council wanted the rental housing. So we held to what we thought was important and I think we did something good. If you ask the average person in the West End today, my guess is they'd be very supportive of the end product. I believe it is beautiful rental housing.

Was this a case where you didn't do enough of the kind of thorough community consultation that is your firm's hallmark?
We failed on that one. I was arrogant in that I assumed everyone understood how important rental housing was and I don't think we did enough to articulate that need. Our client undertook a year of public consultation prior to our being hired for the Honest Ed's site and the goodwill we now have in the Bloor and Bathurst community is the direct result of that authentic effort to listen.

At the Park Plaza when you presented the project over 600 people attended and you could feel the sense of suspicion in the room dissolve.
We had applause at the end. I had my life threatened, but I've never had applause. On Twitter that night we were the third-highest trending topic in Toronto and, unbelievably, 97 percent of the Twitter comments were positive. I think that's a testament not only to the values the project is espousing, but also to the consultation by Westbank. Our team listened and came forward with design that reflected what many people told us they hoped to see.

The original conception of this book was that it be a series of spoken letters to a young architect, which is an idea you had taken from the poet Rainer Maria Rilke. Who would you want your architect to read?
I would say start with history rather than a specific person. The best way of predicting the future is to know the past. It's obvious. The architect's role was once the articulation of God's presence on earth. So there was an important spiritual component, and the value of that articulation was taken very seriously in society. The average building in the medieval period was built by craftsmen and not by architects. Architect's skills were honed to divine our relationship with the cosmos and important festivals, which celebrated the seasonal rituals of daily life. As modernity progressed and the spiritual component of our lives was separated from the powers that run our society, the architect's role transformed. In modernity, we began to see architects being able to design any building typology. We became specialists—tradesmen rather than poets who divined to illuminate god's presence on earth. In that context, our role has been diminished.

So how does the architect re-gain that role in a meaningful way?
For me, it is a humanist set of values that need to be espoused by those of

us who care about this planet from a culturally sustainable point of view, who care about those who don't have affordable housing, who care about drug policy that affects mental health issues. How do you go about absorbing that role and re-interpreting it in your daily life and in your practice? It's not an easy task. But the young architect doesn't have to become a Renaissance man or woman again, each of us has to find the place that makes sense, each of us has to contribute to a collective discussion. What are the things that matter in your life? If it's an aesthetic thing, then there is room for people to do boutiques for clothing designers. If it's spiritual, there is church architecture. And if you want to change the planet for the better then you have to engage environmental issues, you have to deal with housing and large societal issues. You have to see yourself as part of the team that includes the people who are running our society, the people who are in charge of the money, and the people who we elect to represent us. So how do you have a dialogue among all these different players and see the form-giver as someone who isn't just taking orders? The form-giver has the potential to become someone who proposes innovative solutions and is willing to take a leadership role in the community.

So your architect, if he or she is doing a good job, is necessarily an activist?

Yes, and they have their eyes wide open. If you want to be effective and break through the Kafka paradigm, then you have to educate yourself about a myriad of issues. It's not only history, it's also the bureaucracy and policy. It's economics and pro-formas for developers; it's technology and environmental issues. No one person can do all these things, so in our practice there are 50 architects. I have people who are experts in different components and they become a team who then partners with experts outside the practice. You have to see it as a collaborative effort now. It is an orchestra.

One of the notable things about the Henriquez Partnership is that you've been involved in building all those things you mention, from boutiques to churches. It is a broadly based practice.

I think that stems from my father's history of being a practitioner in a small city that had a very fragile economy for a long time, and having the dexterity and ability to move around and try different things. That started out as a necessity for survival and what it taught me was we can do anything if we put together the right team.

Would you have your young architect look at specific practitioners, or is their job to have their eyes wide open and look at everything that is being built?

It's all in front of you in your daily life. Every building you walk into has a story, every structure you visit around the world came from some societal order that you can investigate, or some values and conditions that brought it into being. The more you understand the intentions of something, the better insights you have. So not only is the embodied experience of something important, so is understanding why it came into being, how it was greeted by the world, and how it was re-used over time.

So you wouldn't have your young architect seek out buildings made by Renzo Piano, or Rem Koolhaas, or Frank Gehry?

The rock stars are smart, there is no question about that, but there are only a handful of them. I have a profound respect for some of their work and a lot can be learned from visiting their buildings. It's just that they only participate in a fraction of what is built in society and the structures that really matter are the ones we live in every day, shop in every day, that we give birth in and in which we bury people. There is no afterlife in the paradigm shift announced by modernity. There is this life. And in this life we want to create as just, as meaningful, and as inclusive a society as possible, and tread as lightly on the planet as we can. So given all those humanistic goals, how do you go about adapting your reality to be more in sync with things that matter?

I often quote, to my continuing dismay because I think it might be true, an observation made by W.H. Auden, who said that 'poetry makes nothing happen'. Does architecture make things happen?
I think it does. But it can only happen if society as a whole will fundamentally allow it to happen. That can be done through a collective agreement; it can be done through a Machiavellian series of deals in a boardroom, or it can be done through some sort of benevolent despot who decides what is the best thing for society. There are all sorts of mechanisms through which architecture comes into being. The ideal one is democratic but it isn't always. Some of our most cherished leaders did things that were unpopular because they thought they were in the best interests of society as a whole and, over time, history has been kind to them. You don't know if you'll be on the right side of history, but this is where the question of one's ethics is essential. You have to look inside yourself for what matters in life, what you want from your personal story, and what matters within your community. This is an authentic search for a personal narrative.

In the Woodward's book you said, 'The biggest failure of your profession is the inability to have faith in itself and in humanity to make a difference.' Would you be as harsh on your profession now as you were six years ago?
I'm probably a little more cynical now than I was then. But the environmental movement has really taken off. There is a strong consensus that global warming is real and that protecting the planet's ecosystems is an urgent reality. So there are some quantifiable tasks at hand that our generation can work towards, be it cycling or culture or alternative energy, and all sorts of daily life activities, which can affect both the future of our

planet and the quality of people's lives. But what is missing is the glue that binds those humanistic values to a larger poetic or spiritual aspiration and that still relies upon an artist. It is a tall order to see society uniting all of them and I don't know if you can find it in one practice or one architect. There is so much concern within our own practice to do the right thing that I worry the poetic dimension gets lost. And sometimes the poetry comes out in the funniest places. We were doing this pavilion at the entrance to TELUS Garden, which is the headquarters for TELUS, the huge communications company. We have this amazing structure that is somewhere between a prehistoric dinosaur, the ribs of a whale, an old boat hull, and some sort of timber gothic cathedral. It's this block-long pavilion that defines the entrance to the building and it has become the talk of Vancouver because it is so 'other.' The building does everything you're supposed to do that's right for the planet. It is the first LEED-platinum office building in Vancouver, it is an office tower with windows that open, it has radiant ceilings, and it is very modern. So in that spirit I decided to do this modernist space frame thing over the plaza. Ian Gillespie loved it but the other half of the client group was Darren Entwistle, the head of TELUS Garden and he had a very different aesthetic. He is a brilliant, powerful, and articulate man and he could hold up the whole project because, after all, it is their building. Darren wanted something "west coast gothic" and he talked about the need for recognizing First Nations in the entry design and a respect for the emotive paintings of Emily Carr. Every time I tried to draw something literally gothic it seemed anachronistic and so inappropriate that I couldn't even present it to Darren and Ian. There is a young man in my office named Payam Ashjae who is incredibly talented at designing while 3D modelling, and he and I would sit together for hours and hours, just experimenting. He would flip things one way, then another. We did 25 designs and finally one stuck. He said, 'What is it?' and I said, 'I don't know.' It's almost like you're inside Moby Dick or in a fictional First Nations forest where the trees are moving.

I would say it is the most challenging design to build and the most unnamable form. And it's the one Darren chose. He loves it, Ian loves it, and so do I. It is a fabulously bizarre thing.

Citizen City is a very particular title. I want you to parse the component parts and give me a sense of how it reflects your architectural practice.
The goal of the book is to articulate to young architects and people interested in urban issues the power of collaboration. I hope the Bloor and Bathurst project becomes a reflection of that, as Woodward's was. The book is about those humanistic aspirations and about citizens or individuals in society participating in a larger dialectic that assumes responsibility for the environment we create. I think a lot of people leave it up to experts; they assume that someone knows what they're doing out there. The reality is that things often happen for no good reason, or they happen for the wrong reasons. They happen because of the power of money or political expediency. The totality of the issues that need to be confronted in order for us to make a meaningful urban landscape aren't examined by enough people. The way we envision our cities as a whole needs to be thoughtfully examined. I don't think the way to go is to legislate community values, however well intentioned they may be. Societal values are constantly changing. The players involved in individual projects vary from site to site and while you have to ensure there is a framework, you also have to ensure that there is the flexibility to do the right thing in each circumstance. It requires vigilance and an ongoing monitoring that can't be fixed with policy and bureaucracy. You can't just put everything in place and have it run. There needs to be enough tenure that you can actually execute your ideas. So this book's message is to articulate how we can work together to make sure that we're doing the best we can to be inclusive, to do the right thing for those who have less, and make sure that the education for our children is

meaningful and useful. I think society should be judged by how we treat our least fortunate.

The general question you pose in the book is which projects work and why do they?
It's just heavy lifting and hard work. If things work out, it is because we rarely give up. This kind of stamina is required in any profession. If there is a lesson to the young architect, it's not some divine inspiration or some very specific argument you make that will cause something to come to fruition. It's that every day you have to give one hundred percent of your attention and you have to be critical and creative enough to re-examine the methods you're using, and flexible enough to adapt them given changing environments. It could be that on a specific site the zoning is extremely rigid and you can only challenge certain parts of it, or it could be that you want to look at the whole thing and you realize it is going to take years and years. You have to make a judgment call from project to project about the likelihood of success and the merits of the thing you're doing, and whether it's worth going to the wall for or not. But perseverance is everything. I've met all sorts of architects who are more talented than us but they may not have the work ethic and their potential is never realized. That said, they often have a more balanced and happy life.

But the projects you have had difficulty with don't show any less perseverance than the ones that were less difficult to realize.
On some of them, like Stop-gap housing, I called it a day. We developed this amazing proposal with the Portland Hotel Society and Ian Gillespie and other contractors and consultants. As a city, we were going to end homelessness before the Olympics because no one wanted to be embarrassed on CNN. In the beginning of any project I get this sort of

evangelical blindness where I believe that because we are doing the right thing, everyone is going to follow suit. I showed it to the head of housing for the City, Cameron Gray, who is one of my most respected colleagues over the years, and he looked at me as if I were insane and said, 'This doesn't work,' and I said, 'Why not?' So he told me, 'Well, the poverty activists on the left aren't going to support you because you're not giving them permanent housing, you're going to put all the people in the non-profit housing sector out of a job and the people in the neighbourhoods where you're going to put 'encampments' aren't going to be happy. It's a clusterfuck— it doesn't work.' It would actually get everyone off the street and it would only cost 50 million dollars to get rid of all the homelessness in Vancouver. So it was cheap and it could happen fast. The site the City chose for a potential prototype was adjacent to Chinatown, right beside a viaduct where many homeless people were already camping out. It was right up against Strathcona, which is slowly becoming gentrified with young families and professionals, who were not going to be excited about this. Also, there has been a gradual spiraling down of Chinatown's success and so the Chinese community saw this as a kick in the head. It had no legs. I made the judgment that it was time to call it a day.

I want to know if the case studies in the book are a uniquely Vancouver story, or is it possible to do what you've done in other cities?
These are uniquely Vancouver stories but at the same time the principles could easily be applied in other places. The project would have to be in a city where the profit inherent in the development process is sufficiently robust that extra money can be harnessed to do something of value to the community. There has to be a Community Amenity Contribution of substance to do something and that only arises if there is a very healthy economy and if the development process is very profitable. That applies in a city like Toronto. What we call the Community Amenity Contribution they

call Section 37. But in Toronto it only captures 18 percent of the lift, whereas in Vancouver we capture 75 to 80 percent of the lift in the land value created in a re-zoning. It tells you something about how different the societal values are in the two cities. Developers in Toronto are benefitting an extra 60 percent profit just on increased land value they're not even paying for. Society grants them this additional density and they give back less than in Vancouver. You can argue what the appropriate number should be in many ways, but 18 percent isn't as significant a number as 75 percent. In Vancouver it has been going on for years and it has been tested. There's two ways of calculating the Community Amenities in Vancouver. One is paying 75 to 80 percent of the lift based on the value of the land— so you take the appraised value of the density at $150 a square foot, you multiply it times the extra density, you take 75 percent of that, and cut them a cheque. Or you do some good deeds within or around the project. The other one is a pro-forma method where you show the actual value of that density on your specific project. It might be less than 75 percent, or it could be more, depending on how much it increases the value of the land. Sometimes developers who do better architecture or provide better public spaces will argue that quality in the construction is something that should come out of that lift value, or in going from LEED gold to platinum there could be an environmental upcharge component that is often seen as part of the contribution to the larger community.

Is any city an urban laboratory where experiments get tried, or is there more flexibility for the kind of experimentation you have done in Vancouver than in other places?
I think a lot of it has to do with the absence of significant history in Vancouver (save for First Nations history). It's like the Wild West. It's just over a hundred years old, so compared to Rome, it's a brand new city. And less history means fewer rules and regulations, more openness, and a less

hierarchical society. The amount of money pouring in from Asia has an impact on a small city like Vancouver. Vancouver real estate is like a safety deposit box for money from China, and that alone inflates the value. I can't think of a better and safer place to store your money. We're doing the Oakridge Redevelopment right now, a 1.8 billion dollar project, and there will be some 500 units of social housing. What that housing will pay for is a new daycare facility, a library, and a community centre and park. The project couldn't happen unless you had that kind of investment and that amount of money coming in.

Let's go back to the Children of Woodward's. I want to start with the Remand Centre your father built in 1971. There must be a particular pleasure in turning a jail into social housing for the very aboriginal population that in the past would have been inmates in the remand facility?

It's a special project for both of us. In the '60s there were certain aspirations in which they thought people could be incarcerated more ethically and this was an attempt to do it, with Ping-Pong and pool tables and terraces that faced the mountains. The endeavour was not so successful and the building had been vacant for many years. When the mayor came to power and promised to end homelessness, we saw an opportunity to propose something to BC Housing because we had this empty building. At the time for 10 million dollars —I think its closer to 20 million now— we could house over a hundred people. We proposed it in 2008 and it will open at the end of this year, so it will have taken eight long years. But the poetic dimension of turning a prison into social housing gives me goosebumps.

That building matters to you a great deal, doesn't it? The scale of the project is not the thing that determines your interest?

No. We lost a lot of money on that project. What they pay us every month doesn't cover our staff costs. But we do it because we believe it matters. Our practice has a number of projects along the same lines, like the Immigrant Services Society Welcome House, a building to temporarily house immigrants who are refugees from the war-torn places in the world, where there is genocide and persecution. Canada still takes in some of those people and the work to integrate them into our society is extremely important. A group of non-profits is moving into the centre to deal with everything from victims of torture to new language services. There are classrooms, there are offices, and there's a banking facility where they'll be taught how to bank. It is a prototype for a one-stop immigrant-welcoming centre that doesn't exist anywhere else in the world.

The idea for the conversion of the Remand Centre came at a particularly low time for the firm, didn't it? Was it a make-work project for your staff?
Yes. In 2008 we were about 33 people and the whole world seemed to fall apart. I had close to a million dollars in accounts receivable and no one was paying us because the banks were not advancing on loans. But I'm a saver and we had put money away for a rainy day and that rainy day came. It was a hard time because we still had to lay off five people, but then we set about creating make-work projects, hoping to inspire governments to fund them. Stop-gap Housing and the Bike Bridge were designed at that time, and the Remand Centre re-birth was also developed during that period. Luckily our financial drought only lasted eight months and today we're about 60 staff and growing.

In the case of the York Theatre Revitalization the building was close to demolition and you got a 120-day reprieve to save the building from being knocked down.
This was another Jim Green project. The York Theatre is one of the last vaudeville theatres in Vancouver. It is interesting what happens and what

doesn't happen. I guess the new Council coming in saw the project as a great equalizer because, compared to the West Side, there was a lack of cultural institutions on the East Side. So the heritage community, the neighbourhood, and the arts community were all on the same side. But the economic deal shouldn't have happened. Traditionally one-third would have come from each of the federal government, the Province, and the City, but this was almost entirely done with community heritage density and a bit of federal money that came in later. At the end of the day, it turned out beautifully for everyone involved. The old vaudeville theatres didn't have lobbies because you would go in and out anytime between noon to midnight. So there was a little sliver of land on the front where we did a very narrow lobby, it is really long and skinny, and we made it look like a proscenium arch or curtain being pulled away. There are beautiful locally made glazed red tiles on the outside, so it is a metaphorical curtain being pulled back with a glass façade behind. The spectators at intermission become the actors in an urban theatre of people viewed from the street.

What about the Toronto project? How is the Vancouver architect who knows that city and its operations inside and out, finding being a newbie in a different city?
That's a good question. I wouldn't have taken on the project if I didn't think there was a sympathetic relationship between our values and history, the community we're working with and, of course, the aspirations of our client. Westbank started a year earlier doing a lot of the things we've been doing with them for a decade in terms of reaching out to the entire neighbourhood, to the non-profits, the civic officials and the residents associations—all the things we do in Vancouver. So it is a matter of taking the lessons learned at home over a very long time and applying them here. The nice thing is that it's not the convention here—community outreach

isn't typical for a developer or an architect in Toronto. It is a very different landscape and so we're being well received, so far. It's surprising on one level but it is also very reassuring because you get the sense that everyone is yearning for the same things, they want to retain their sense of community, they want to be engaged in the process, they want an equitable society, and everybody wants to have exciting local retail opportunities that aren't big boxing. They want their communities to reflect their values. These are the values upon which our design practice is grounded, so it's not that surprising that they're being embraced, but it is rare to feel such a sense of appreciation for our efforts.

So many of your projects are involved directly with the arts. You seem to accept them as an integral part of any serious mixed-use project.
I grew up in a family where making art was like eating breakfast. It was one of the important things in life. For me it is not something that is added on. The most poignant example I can think of was that Jim Green would always run opera in the Downtown Eastside out of this community bank we built together. He would get the Vancouver Opera to come down and sing on Saturday for all the residents. Jim would say, 'Listen, they need food and they need shelter and they also need culture. They need to be uplifted and to be touched by the spiritual dimensions of the universe.' Everyone needs the same things, right? Whether you're rich or poor. Art isn't only for the wealthy. The nice thing about the projects we do is that we always incorporate not only public art, but we try to find ways to include cultural components that can support the arts. So for Bloor and Bathurst we're talking about doing artists' studios, for Woodward's we have a centre for performing arts, for 6th & Fir, we have artists' studios. Artists are meaningful and important people in a healthy creative community—they take a lot of risks in their daily life and they struggle with subsistence and

need to be supported. Not every artist is as successful as Stan Douglas (I am a big fan). Artists at the beginning of their careers are the ones who need the most help. Whenever we can, we encourage clients to include studio space.

You take an especially active role in your projects. We talked earlier about the architect as an aesthetic and civic activist. It isn't simply that people come to you with a project, but you also decide to go after projects that you want to initiate?

That's an important message. I know most architectural firms have marketing staff that constantly go after Request for Proposals. That work is usually published—it is government work or from a developer, and the project has generally been fully envisioned. There is a program, a budget and a site. Basically, you're coming in and you're solving a problem by adding form to an idea that has been around, maybe for many years. I believe that the more the architect can be involved in earlier phases, in site selection, or in figuring out what a group really needs, the better. Or go back even a step further. Some of the more interesting projects in the book are trying to solve issues that don't have clients yet, ideas that come to you from others, and they need help to figure out how to solve their own problems. Young architects should get out there and participate in society, let people know who you are, meet as many people as you can. There were years when I went for lunch with a different person almost every day. I thought, 'Who do I want to meet?' And I'd make a list of the 50 people and I'd go for lunch. You get to know your community and you get to know the human network of your city. The critical message is you can't do anything alone in your studio. You need to find the partners and the advocates and the projects that matter to you and to your personal vision of the world.

So it is still critical because the discourse around the idea of what could be done is equally important?

Yes, but the discourse has to be in the public realm. It can't be in your studio. Do it in your studio if you want but make sure you call up the five reporters who are on that list of people you had lunch with and say, 'Listen, this is a really important idea. I'm going to end homelessness and I'm going to do it with this crazy stop-gap housing idea I have. Everyone is going to live in these portables and I'm going to paint them different colours'. And you talk to the experts about mental health issues for homeless people, how they can't go down a corridor, so we need to make individual front doors for each unit (a micro-motel concept), and what are they going to do with their shopping carts? And food is going to come in on food trucks and you find someone who can run a model on the operating costs and, little by little, you gain enough rigour that it is not just a theoretical project done by a bunch of architecture students. It actually may have some legs. Then you take it to engineering professionals and a very friendly construction company that has some credibility and you find a developer who's willing to finance it and you piece this project together so that, as ridiculous as it sounds, it has as much gravitas as possible, so that the world will at least look at it seriously. When I came out of architectural school I wanted very badly to be an academic who taught. That didn't turn out to be in the cards. What I hope I'm doing is teaching in another way. I'm teaching by doing.

The preceding interview was conducted in Toronto on March 30, 2015.

Bibliography

"1401 Comox - St John's Church." West End Neighbours. N.p., 13 June 2012. Web. 28 July 2014.

"2013 Cost of Living Survey Rankings." Mercer's 2013 Cost of Living City Rankings. Mercer, n.d. Web. 25 July 2014.

Adams, Michael. *Fire and Ice: The United States, Canada and the Myth of Converging Values.* Canada: Penguin, 2009. Print.

Alini, Erica. "Vancouver–the most livable city?" *Maclean's.* Rogers Media, 14 Sept. 2011. Web. 24 July 2014.

Amzaleg, Ben. "Blog: 60 West Cordova Street." Web blog post. *Ben Amzaleg Blog.* Ben Amzaleg Personal Real Estate, 30 Oct. 2010. Web. 29 July 2014.

"Analysis of the Canadian Immigrant Labour Market, 2008 to 2011." *Statistics Canada.* Canada.ca, 19 June 2013. Web. 17 July 2014.

Austin, James E. *The Collaboration Challenge: How Nonprofits and Businesses Succeed Through Strategic Alliances.* San Francisco: Jossey-Bass, 2000. Print.

Axelsson, Robert, Per Angelstam, Erik Degerman, Sara Teitelbaum, Kjell Andersson, Marine Elbakidze, and Marcus K. Drotz. "Social and Cultural Sustainability: Criteria, Indicators, Verifier Variables for Measurement and Maps for Visualization to Support Planning." *Ambio* 42.2 (2013): 215-228. Print.

Bagli, Charles. "Developers End Fight Blocking 2 More Luxury Towers in Midtown." *New York Times.* New York Times, 15 Oct. 2013. Web. 17 July 2014.

Beasley, Larry. Personal interview. 26 Aug. 2013.

Berelowitz, Lance. *Dream City: Vancouver and the Global Imagination.* Vancouver: Douglas, 2005. Print.

Birnie, Peter. "Part three: View on Vancouver's live music venues." *Vancouver Sun.* Pacific Newspaper Group, 26 Aug. 2009. Web. 28 July 2014.

—. "Wall Financial, City of Vancouver, team to save Commercial Drive's historic York Theatre from demolition." *Vancouver Sun.* Pacific Newspaper Group, 2 Feb. 2009. Web. 24 July 2014.

Bula, Frances. "Bike-only bridge debate breaks out." Web blog post. *State of Vancouver: Frances Bula on city life and politics.* France Bula RSS, 4 July 2009. Web. 29 July 2014.

—. "Gallery should stay put, advocates say." *Globe and Mail.* Globe and Mail, 5 Mar. 2010. Web. 29 July 2014.

—. "Vancouver's architecture under the spotlight." *Globe and Mail.* Globe and Mail, 19 Jan. 2010. Web. 25 July 2014.

—. "Woodward's developer tries new experiment in affordable housing." Web blog post. *State of Vancouver: Frances Bula on city life and politics.* Frances Bula RSS, 26 July 2010. Web. 29 July 2014.

"Businesses Have a Role in Solving Homelessness." 3 Ways to Home. Greater Vancouver Regional Steering Committee on Homelessness. Issue 16 (2010) Print.

Campbell, Charles. "Saying goodbye to the Ridge Theatre." *Georgia Straight.* Vancouver Free Press, 21 Jan. 2013. Web. 28 July 2014.

Canada. British Columbia. *Community Amenity Contributions: Balancing Community Planning, Public Benefits and Housing Affordability.* Ministry of Community, Sport and Cultural Development, 2014. Web.

Canada. British Columbia. *Premier Opens Canada's First Community Court.* Office of the Premier, 6 September 2008. Web.

Canada. British Columbia. *Society Selected For Housing at Former Remand Centre Site.* Ministry of Natural Gas Development and Minister Responsible for Housing, 13 October 2011. Web.

Canada. British Columbia. *Vancouver's Downtown Community Court.* Ministry of Attorney General, 6 September 2008. Web.

Canada. British Columbia. *Vancouver's Downtown Community Court First Anniversary.* Ministry of Attorney General, 18 September 2009. Web.

Canada. City of Vancouver. *2012 Annual Report on Development Cost Levies.*
Administrative Report: Supports Item No. 5. Vancouver: Vancouver.ca, 2013. Web.

Canada. City of Vancouver. *Capital Grant to Immigrant Services Society of BC for a
Housing Development of 26 Units (with 98 lockable rooms) at 2610 Victoria Drive.*
Administrative Report: A3. Vancouver: Vancouver.ca, 2013. Web.

Canada. City of Vancouver. *CD-1 Rezoning – 1569 West 6th Avenue. Policy Report
Development and Building:* P6. Vancouver: Vancouver.ca, 2010. Web.

Canada. City of Vancouver. *CD-1 Rezoning: 2610 Victoria Drive – ISSBC. Policy Report
Development and Building:* P2. Vancouver: Vancouver.ca, 2012. Web.

Canada. City of Vancouver. Director of Planning. *Rental Incentive Guidelines.
Planning - By-Law Administrative Bulletin.* 15 May 2012. Print.

Canada. City of Vancouver. *Grant Request for 211 Gore Avenue (former Remand Center).*
Administrative Report: A2. Vancouver: Vancouver.ca, 2011. Web.

Canada. City of Vancouver. Housing Policy Community Services Group. 2007
Survey of Low-Income Housing in the Downtown Core. Vancouver: Vancouver.ca,
2007. Web.

Canada. City of Vancouver. Mayor's Task Force on Housing Affordability. *Bold
Ideas Towards an Affordable City.* Vancouver: Vancouver.ca, 2012. Web.

Canada. City of Vancouver. *Option to Purchase 639 Commercial Drive (York Theatre)
and Lease of 639 Commercial Drive to the Vancouver East Cultural Centre.*
Administrative Report: Supports Item No. 4. Vancouver: Vancouver.ca, 2011. Web.

Canada. City of Vancouver. *Public Hearing: Summary and Recommendation. Rezoning:*
1401 Comox Street. Vancouver: Vancouver.ca, 2012. Web.

Canada. City of Vancouver. *Public Hearing: Summary and Recommendation. Rezoning:*
1569 West 6th Avenue. Vancouver: Vancouver.ca, 2010. Web.

Canada. City of Vancouver. *Public Hearing: Summary and Recommendation. Rezoning:*
2610 Victoria Drive – ISSBC. Vancouver: Vancouver.ca, 2012. Web.

Canada. City of Vancouver. *Public Hearing: Summary and Recommendation. Rezoning/
Heritage Designation/Heritage revitalization agreement (HRA): 639 Commercial Drive
(York Theatre).* Vancouver: Vancouver.ca, 2011. Web.

Canada. City of Vancouver. *Results of Short Term Incentives for Rental (STIR) Program Presentation to City Council.* PowerPoint Presentation. City of Vancouver Staff, 27 March 2012. Web.

Canada. City of Vancouver. *Secured Market Rental Housing Policy. Policy Report Social Development. Supports Item No. 2.* Vancouver: Vancouver.ca, 2012. Web.

Canada. City of Vancouver. *Temporary Protection of the York Theatre - 639 Commercial Drive. Administrative Report: Support Item No. 1.* Vancouver: Vancouver.ca, 2008. Web.

Canada. City of Vancouver. *Vancouver's Housing and Homelessness Strategy 2012 – 2021, A Home for Everyone.* 2012. Print.

Canada. City of Vancouver. *Vancouver's Housing and Homelessness Strategy: Secured Marketing Rental Housing Policy.* 2012. Print.

Canada. City of Vancouver. *West End Community Plan.* 20 November 2013. Print.

Canada. City of Vancouver. *West End: Exploring the Community. Community Profile 2012.* Vancouver.ca, 2012.

Canada. Metro Vancouver. "2011 Census Bulletin #1 Population and Dwelling Counts." Metro Vancouver, 2011. Web.

Canada. Metro Vancouver. "2011 National Household Survey – Bulletin #6 Immigration and Cultural Diversity." Metro Vancouver, 2011. Web.

Canada. Metro Vancouver. "Metro Vancouver Housing Data Book." Metro Vancouver, Dec. 2015. Web.

"Canadian Human Rights Commission." CHRC. Canada.ca, n.d. Web. 17 July 2014.

"Central Presbyterian Church – Vancouver, BC, Canada." Central Presbyterian Church, n.d. Web. 28 July 2014.

Chan, Damon. Personal interview. 01 Nov. 2013 and 07 Mar. 2014.

Chodikoff, Ian. "An Ethical Plan." *Canadian Architect.* 1 Feb. 2007: 38-41. Print.

"City Approves Artist Studio Space." Web blog post. *Alliance for Arts + Culture Blog.* Alliance for Arts + Culture, 18 Apr. 2012. Web. 28 July 2014.

"City of Vancouver Invests in 95 New Units of Affordable Housing for the Downtown Eastside." *Vancouver Mayor's Office.* City of Vancouver, 4 May 2011. Web. 28 July 2014.

"City-owned industrial spaces become artist studios." City of Vancouver. Vancouver.ca, n.d. Web. 28 July 2014.

Cole, Yolande. "Vancouver council approves tower for 1401 Comox Street in the West End." *Georgia Straight*. Vancouver Free Press, 27 June 2012. Web. 28 July 2014.

—. "Vancouver marks opening of York Theatre on Commercial Drive." *Georgia Straight*. Vancouver Free Press, 5 Dec. 2013. Web. 24 July 2014.

"Community Amenity Contributions." *City of Vancouver*. Vancouver.ca, n.d. Web. 20 July 2014.

"Community court opens on Vancouver's Downtown Eastside - British Columbia - CBC News." *CBCnews.ca*. CBC/Radio Canada, 10 Sept. 2008. Web. 28 July 2014.

"Constitution Acts, 1867 to 1982." *Legislative Services Branch*. Canada.ca, n.d. Web. 16 July 2014.

Corburn, Jason. *Street Science Community Knowledge and Environmental Health Justice*. Cambridge: MIT, 2005. Print.

Cotten, Marya N. and Gail A. Lasprogata. "Corporate Citizenship & Creative Collaboration: Best Practices for Cross-Sector Partnerships." *Journal of Law, Business & Ethics* 18 (Winter 2012): 9-39. Print.

Coupland, Douglas. *City of Glass: Douglas Coupland's Vancouver*. Vancouver: Douglas, 2000. Print.

Coutts, Matthew. "Is Vancouver really Canada's most livable city?" *Yahoo News Canada*. N.p., 29 Aug. 2013. Web. 18 July 2014.

"Creating and preserving market rental housing." *City of Vancouver*. Vancouver.ca, n.d. Web. 28 July 2014.

"Critics attack mayor's False Creek cycling bridge plan." *Canada.com*. Vancouver Courier, 8 July 2009. Web. 29 July 2014.

"Cycling in Vancouver." *City of Vancouver*. Vancouver.ca, n.d. Web. 29 July 2014.

Demers, Charles. *Vancouver Special*. Vancouver: Arsenal Pulp, 2009. Print.

"Development Cost Levies." *City of Vancouver*. Vancouver.ca, n.d. Web. 20 July 2014.

Ditmars, Hadani. "Vancouver architect Gregory Henriquez takes on a post-Woodward's task." *Globe and Mail*. Globe and Mail, 2 Sept. 2011. Web. 24 July 2014.

Eidse, James, Mari Fujita, Joey Giaimo, and Christa Min, eds. *Vancouver Matters*. Vancouver: Blueimprint, 2008. Print.

Enright, Robert, ed. *Body Heat: The Story of the Woodward's Redevelopment*. Vancouver: Blueimprint, 2010. Print.

Evans, Liz. Personal interview. 23 July 2013.

Fainstein, Susan S. *The Just City*. Ithaca: Cornell UP, 2010. Print.

Gaumont, Adam. "City takes the middle road on Burrard Bridge." *BCLiving*. Canada Wide Media, 28 May 2009. Web. 29 July 2014.

Gibbon, John Murray. *Canadian Mosaic: The Making of a Northern Nation*. Toronto: McClelland, 1938. Print.

Gillespie, Ian. Personal interview. 08 Nov. 2013.

Glaeser, Edward L. *Triumph of the City: How Our Greatest Invention Makes Us Richer, Smarter, Greener, Healthier, and Happier*. New York: Penguin, 2011. Print.

Gold, Kerry. "A garden in the sky in the heart of Vancouver." *Globe and Mail*. Globe and Mail, 28 Nov. 2011. Web. 25 July 2014.

—. "A plan to turn a former jail into rental housing." *Globe and Mail*. Globe and Mail, 22 Dec. 2011. Web. 25 July 2014.

Grdadolnik, Helena. "Crosstown Examined." Canadian Architect (Jan. 2006): 20-25. Print.

"Greenest City: 2020 Action Plan." *City of Vancouver* (2011) Print.

Griffin, Kevin. "Switch to biofuel heating may be one green footstep for Vancouver." *Vancouver Sun*. Pacific Newspaper Group, 19 Feb. 2014. Web. 24 July 2014.

Habitat for Humanity Society of Greater Vancouver. Memorandum of Understanding to Cordova Housing Holdings Inc. Vancouver, Canada. 10 March 2011. Print.

Hansen, Darah. "Vancouver affordable housing strategy aims to add rental units, ease rates." *Vancouver Sun*. Pacific Newspaper Group, 27 Sept. 2012. Web. 25 July 2014.

—. "Vancouver rental-housing incentive program put to the test." *Vancouver Sun*. Pacific Newspaper Group, 21 Feb. 2013. Web. 28 July 2014.

Henegar, Hilary. "Burrard, bikes and Vancouver's long-term livability goals." *BCLiving*. Canada Wide Media, 13 July 2009. Web. 29 July 2014.

"Heritage Vancouver 2008 Top Ten Endangered Sites." *Heritage Vancouver Society*. Heritage Vancouver Society, n.d. Web. 28 July 2014.

Hiebert, Daniel, and Kathy Sherrell. "The Integration and Inclusion of Newcomers in British Columbia." *Metropolis British Columbia Working Paper Series* 09 - 11 (Nov. 2009). Print.

Hiebert, Daniel. "A New Residential Order?: The Social Geography of Visible Minority and Religious Groups in Montreal, Toronto, and Vancouver in 2031." *Citizenship & Immigration Canada* (July 2012) Print.

—. "The Economic Integration of Immigrants in Metropolitan Vancouver." *Metropolis British Columbia Working Papers Series* 09-08 (Sept. 2009) Print.

Hodge, Jarrah. "A Backwards Approach to Homelessness." *Vancouver Observer*. Observer Media Group, 13 Oct. 2009. Web. 29 July 2014.

"Homeless youth pushed out for 2010 Games - British Columbia - CBC News." *CBCnews*. CBC/Radio Canada, 13 Feb. 2011. Web. 29 July 2014.

Hui, Stephen. "Homelessness doubled ahead of Vancouver Olympics, report shows." *Georgia Straight*. Vancouver Free Press, 3 Dec. 2009. Web. 29 July 2014.

Hume, Mark. "Vancouver plans to create affordable studio space for artists." *Globe and Mail*. Globe and Mail, 12 June 2012. Web. 24 July 2014.

Hyslop, Lucy. "Winter Olympics on slippery slope after Vancouver crackdown on homeless." *Guardian*. Guardian News and Media, 3 Feb. 2010. Web. 29 July 2014.

"Incentives for Developers: Transferable Heritage Density Bonuses." *City of Vancouver*. Vancouver.ca, n.d. Web. 20 July 2014.

Jacobs, Ned. "22-storey tower at 1401 Comox Street would degrade livability in West End." *Georgia Straight*. Vancouver Free Press, 11 Mar. 2010. Web. 28 July 2014.

Jackson, Gillan. Personal interview. 24 July 2013.

Jobin, Garry. Personal interview. 06 August 2013.

"Justice Reforms Initiatives." *British Columbia*. Provincial Government of British Columbia, n.d. Web. 28 July 2014.

Kristof, Nicholas. "It's Now the Canadian Dream." *New York Times*. New York Times, 14 May 2014. Web. 17 July 2014.

Kupferschmidt, Stanislav. "The gentrification plot thickens at 60 W. CORDOVA…" *Vancouver Media Co-op*. Vancouver Media Co-op, 1 Oct. 2010. Web. 29 July 2014.

Lagueux, Maurice. "Ethics versus Aesthetics in Architecture." *The Philosophical Forum* 35.2 (2004): 117-133. Print.

Lasprogata, Gail A., and Marya N. Cotten. "Contemplating Enterprise: The Business and Legal Challenges of Social Entrepreneurship." American Business Law Journal 41.1 (Fall 2003): 67-113. Print.

Lederman, Marsha. "Giving architects their due." *Globe and Mail*. Globe and Mail, 13 Jan. 2010. Web. 29 July 2014.

—. "Rebirth of a century-old B.C. theatre signals sea change for the arts." *Globe and Mail*. Globe and Mail, 30 Nov. 2013. Web. 24 July 2014.

Lee, Jeff. "Vancouver Mayor Gregor Robertson re-elected with full council slate." *Vancouver Sun*. Pacific Newspaper Group, 20 Nov. 2011. Web. 19 Mar. 2013.

Leidl, Patricia. "Vancouver: prosperity and poverty make uneasy bedfellows in world's most 'liveable' city." UNFPA, 2007.

Leiren-Young, Mark. "New New York: theatre a celebration of cultural heritage." *Vancouver Sun*. Pacific Newspaper Group, 2 Dec. 2013. Web. 24 July 2014.

Leonhardt, David, and Kevin Quealy. "The American Middle Class Is No Longer the World's Richest." *New York Times*. New York Times, 22 Apr. 2014. Web. 17 July 2014.

Leung, Ho Hon. "Canadian Multiculturalism in the 21st Century: Emerging Challenges and Debates." *Canadian Ethnic Studies Journal* 43.3 (2011): 19-33. Print.

Levitz, Stephanie. "Homelessness in Canada Report: Add $46 A Year Per Canadian to Housing Budget, End Homelessness" Huffington Post Canada. TheHuffingtonPost.com, 29 October 2014. Web. 30 October 2014.

Lewis, Shauna. "City council approves 1401 Comox tower." *Daily Xtra*. Pink Triangle Press, 27 June 2012. Web. 28 July 2014.

Linden, Isabelle Aube, Marissa Y. Mar, Gregory R. Werker, Kerry Jang, and Michael Krausz. "Research on a Vulnerable Neighborhood - The Vancouver Downtown Eastside from 2001 to 2011." *Journal of Urban Health: Bulletin of the New York Academy of Medicine* 90.3 (2012): 559-573. Print.

"Look out below." *Economist* 4 Feb. 2012. Web. 25 July 2014.

"Mayor's Task Force on Housing Affordability." *City of Vancouver*. Vancouver.ca, n.d. Web. 29 July 2014.

"Median Total Income, by Family Type, by Census Metropolitan Area (All Census Families)." *Statistics Canada*. Canada.ca, 10 Feb. 2013. Web. 17 July 2014.

"Metro Vancouver Housing Market Characterized By Modest Home Sale and Price Increases in 2013." *Real Estate Board of Greater Vancouver*. Real Estate Board of Greater Vancouver, 3 Jan. 2014. Web. 17 July 2014.

Murphy, Elizabeth. "Flawed policies doom Vancouver's old buildings." *Vancouver Sun*. Pacific Newspaper Group, 11 Mar. 2013. Web. 28 July 2014.

"New bike bridge links Richmond, Vancouver - British Columbia - CBC News." *CBCnews*. CBC/Radio Canada, 12 Aug. 2009. Web. 29 July 2014.

"New Park at 6th and Fir." *City of Vancouver*. Vancouver.ca, n.d. Web. 28 July 2014.

Newirth, Rich. "New Strategies to Provide Studio and Creative Space." PowerPoint Presentation to City Council. City of Vancouver Staff, 12 June 2012. Web. 29 July 2014.

"NHS Focus on Geography Series – Vancouver CMA." *Statistics Canada*. Canada.ca, n.d. Web. 17 July 2014.

Noble, Amanda and Lola Oseni. "It's Everybody's Business: Raising the Roof's Private Engagement Project." Canadian Homelessness Research Network, 2013. Web. 29 July 2014.

"One Step Forward... Results of the 2011 Metro Vancouver Homeless Count." 3 Ways to Home. Greater Vancouver Regional Steering Committee on Homelessness, 2012. Web. 28 July 2014.

Pablo, Carlito. "Central Presbyterian Church provides a model for nonmarket rental housing." *Georgia Straight*. Vancouver Free Press, 4 Feb. 2014. Web. 28 July 2014.

—. "Vancouver's Central Presbyterian Church looks at condo development." *Georgia Straight*. Vancouver Free Press, 22 Aug. 2012. Web. 6 Apr. 2013.

Parker, Dara. Personal interview. 09 August 2013.

"Parliamentary Institutions." *Parliament of Canada*. Government of Canada, n.d. Web. 17 July 2014.

Paulsen, Monte. "'Stop Gap Housing' Idea Could Make Big Dent in Homelessness." *Tyee*. N.p., 19 Dec. 2008. Web. 29 July 2014.

"Pedestrian and bike bridge proposed for False Creek - British Columbia - CBC News." *CBCnews*. CBC/Radio Canada, 3 July 2009. Web. 29 July 2014.

Pérez-Gómez, Alberto, et al. *Towards an Ethical Architecture: Issues within the Work of Gregory Henriquez*. Vancouver: Blueimprint, 2006. Print.

Price, Gordon. "A new bridge (and a new option) for False Creek." Web blog post. *Price Tags*. N.p., 6 July 2009. Web. 29 July 2014.

—. "Passerelles of the Year." Web blog post. *Price Tags*. N.p., 5 Jan. 2009. Web. 29 July 2014.

Punter, John. *The Vancouver Achievement: Urban Planning and Design*. Vancouver: UBC, 2003. Print.

QMUNITY, BC's Queer Resource Center. *Strategic Plan*. Canada. 2013-2015.

Quintanar, Paola. "The Dream: Pedestrian and bike only bridges around the world." *BCLiving*. Canada Wide Media, 29 Jan. 2009. Web. 29 July 2014.

"Remand Centre to become homes for BladeRunners youth." BC Housing. BC Housing, 3 Nov. 2011. Web. 18 Nov. 2013.

Rochon, Lisa. "How to build hope? Start with plywood and guts." *Globe and Mail*. Globe and Mail, 6 Mar. 2009. Web. 24 July 2014.

—. "In a big-box world, can the street be saved?" *Globe and Mail*. Globe and Mail, 13 July 2012. Web. 25 July 2014.

Roberts, Joel. "An Olympic Response to Homelessness in London." *Huffington Post*. TheHuffingtonPost.com, 12 Aug. 2012. Web. 29 July 2014.

Robertson, Gregor. "Despite setback, Vancouver's homeless plan is on the right track." *Vancouver Sun*. Pacific Newspaper Group, 28 Apr. 2014. Web. 20 July 2014.

—. "Working to End Homelessness in Vancouver." *Vancouver Mayor's Office*. City of Vancouver, June 2014. Web. 29 July 2014.

Robinson, Matthew. "Two East Vancouver parks to get face lifts." *Vancouver Sun*. Pacific Newspaper Group, 23 Sept. 2013. Web. 28 July 2014.

Schwanke, Dean. "ULI Case Studies: Woodward's." *Urban Land*. Urban Land Institute, 4 Apr. 2014. Web. 25 July 2014.

Sherwell, Philip. "Dark side of Vancouver's Olympic flame." *Telegraph*. Telegraph Media Group, 13 Feb. 2010. Web. 29 July 2014.

Sinoski, Kelly. "Number of people sleeping in Vancouver's streets or on couches more than tripled since 2011 (updated)." *Vancouver Sun*. Pacific Newspaper Group, 23 Apr. 2014. Web. 20 July 2014.

Small, Dan. Personal interview. 23 July and 17 Oct. 2013.

Smith, Charlie. "Vancouver developer Peter Wall brings arts venues to life." *Georgia Straight*. Vancouver Free Press, 4 Dec. 2013. Web. 28 July 2014.

Smith, Jim. Personal interview. 24 July 2103.

Sorensen, Chris. "Crash and Burn." *Maclean's*. Rogers Media, 2 Jan. 2013. Web. 25 July 2014.

Stone, Felicity. "Tate on Howe in Vancouver will incorporate on-site studios and artists' exhibits." *Vancouver Sun*. Pacific Newspaper Group, 24 Nov. 2013. Web. 24 July 2014.

"A Summary of the Global Liveability Ranking and Overview." *Economist Intelligence Unit*. August 2013. Web.

Sutherland, Jim. "Extreme Makeover." *Vancouver Magazine* Apr. 2013. Print.

TELUS. "Dedicated Utility Will Recycle Heat at TELUS Garden, Reducing Co2 Emissions by More Than One Million Kilograms." TELUS Media Releases. TELUS Communications, 28 Feb. 2013. Web. 24 July 2014.

Thompson, Scott. "POLICING VANCOUVER'S MENTALLY ILL: THE DISTURBING TRUTH - Beyond Lost in Translation." *Vancouver Police Department* (2010) Print.

Todd, Douglas. "'State-of-art' Vancouver refugee centre coming amid dramatic changes." *Vancouver Sun*. Pacific Newspaper Group, 20 June 2012. Web. 28 July 2014.

Townsend, Mark. Personal interview. 23 July 2013.

"United Nations Department of Economic and Social Affairs. Population Division." UN News Center. UN, n.d. Web. 27 July 2014.

"The Universal Declaration of Human Rights." *United Nations*. UN, n.d. Web. 26 July 2014.

"Urban Design Panel." *City of Vancouver*. City of Vancouver, n.d. Web. 20 July 2014.

Urbanizta. "1401 Comox rezoning reveals nasty sides of City Hall, developer games in Vancouver." Web blog post. *CityHallWatch*. CityHallWatch Media Foundation, 12 June 2012. Web. 28 July 2014.

"Vancouver rolls out Burrard Bridge bike lanes plan - British Columbia - CBC News." *CBCnews*. CBC/Radio Canada, 23 June 2009. Web. 29 July 2014.

Waddock, Sandra A. "Understanding Social Partnerships: An Evolutionary Model of Partnership Organizations." *Administration & Society* 21.1 (1989): 78-100. Print.

Wall, Bruno. Personal interview. 07 Aug. 2013.

Walton, Dawn. "Vancouver most expensive city in Canada." *Yahoo Finance Canada*. Yahoo! – News Network, 24 July 2013. Web. 17 July 2014.

Werb, Jessica. "Arts groups welcome York Theatre's long-awaited reopening." *Georgia Straight*. Vancouver Free Press, 27 Nov. 2013. Web. 24 July 2014.

"West End community plan approved in Vancouver - British Columbia - CBC News." *CBCnews*. CBC/Radio Canada, 21 Nov. 2013. Web. 28 July 2014.

"Whistler's homeless relocated ahead of Olympics - British Columbia - CBC News." *CBCnews*. CBC/Radio Canada, 8 Jan. 2010. Web. 29 July 2014.

"Why 60 W. Cordova is the unthinkable." *Canada.com.* Vancouver Sun, 13 Nov. 2010. Web. 25 July 2014.

Woodsworth, Ellen. "Ellen Woodsworth: Burrard Bridge cycling trial a huge leap forward." *Georgia Straight.* Vancouver Free Press, 11 July 2009. Web. 29 July 2014.

"World Urbanization Prospects: The 2014 Revision." Department of Economic and Social Affairs. United Nations. New York. 2014

World Commission on Environment and Development. *Our Common Future.* Bungay: Oxford UP, 1987. Print.

Woroch, Patricia. Personal interview. 29 July 2013.

"York Theatre - The Cultch." The Cultch. The Cultch, n.d. Web. 28 July 2014.

Acknowledgments

GREGORY HENRIQUEZ

For Rob, whose love makes all the best things in my life possible,
and sweet Alice, our everything
MARYA COTTEN GOULD

MUCH LIKE the construction of a building, the making of a book is a highly collaborative project. The inspiration for *Citizen City* came from the combination of our desire to share with our authentic hope that architectural practice may still deviate from its current trajectory. The individuals who participated in the projects this book documents are passionate about our urban environment and share the common goal of finding a meaningful way, a new paradigm, to bring into existence cities that reflect a more inclusive society.

Marya Gould walked into my office one day and we immediately knew we were destined to work together. I feel so blessed she chose to help us articulate an ideological context within which to view our projects. She is a serious academic with powerful insights and the rigour to tell our story. It is her book.

Robert Enright is one of my dearest friends and I remain grateful that he continues to show interest in our work. His interview and editing gave the book its final shape. Thank you, Robert, for pushing us to get it out into the world. Your intellect and passion are moving.

Dimiter Savoff, our publisher, has always had the utmost faith in us. This is our fourth book with BlueImprint. Without the grassroots publishing movement of which BlueImprint is a part, small studios like ours would never be able to articulate our mission. Dimiter, your trust has given us the platform to share our ideas. Thank you.

But a few times in a lifetime someone crosses your path and completely changes the trajectory of your story. Ian Gillespie changed my life for the better. After agreeing to pursue and then winning the Woodward's commission, Ian started hiring our studio to land his heritage and amenity density on various new projects. Over the past 12 years, under his visionary leadership we have designed rental housing, affordable condo ownership, civic facilities, private utilities, public art installations, non-market housing, and cultural facilities to name just a few projects. His patronage has enriched our lives, and along the way I made a lifelong friend.

Thank you as well to the following experts, clients, activists, civic leaders, and planners who gave their time to be interviewed by Marya Gould. Their insights provided the necessary context and content to articulate the story of each of the 10 projects:

Larry Beasley, Damon Chan, Liz Evans, Ian Gillespie, Gillan Jackson, Garry Jobin, Dara Parker, Dan Small, Jim Smith, Mark Townsend, Bruno Wall, and Patricia Woroch.

Within the studio of Henriquez Partners there were key individuals who did the large and many small tasks required to piece together this book. All the drawings were done by a young designer named Arnold Wong, and the book would not exist were it not for Kaya Wiggens, whose tenacity kept me focussed and engaged.

Last but never least are the architects, designers, and support staff in our studio that designed, detailed, and supervised the construction of our work. These are talented individuals with the many divergent skills necessary to translate aspirations to concepts, drawings to models. Their skills ultimately result in the physical edifices that people inhabit. I am grateful for their inspired dedication and the perseverance to see things through to final occupancy. This is no small task, but the evidence lives on for generations:

Partners Gregory Henriquez, Richard Henriquez

Directors Peter Wood, Rui Nunes, Patricia Tewfik, Shawn LaPointe, Norman Huth, Christian Ruud, Veronica Gillies

Associates Jaime Dejo, Brock Cheadle, May So, Dallas Hong, Keith Smith

Architects & Designers Payam Ashjae, Milos Begovic, Steve Best, Chris Boldt, Emma Buchanan, Matthew Bulford, Alan Bushby, Jesi Carson, Luke Cho, Quinci Cohen, Michael Cunningham, Maher Elkhaldi, Tara Espey, Rocio Huertas Garcia, Gustavo Gonzalez, Silvia Guzman, Benyi Hu, Nick James, Shadi Jianfar, Chanhoo Kim, Emily Koo, Edgar Leon, Yvonne Liao, Tiphaine Maisonneuve, Babak Manavi, Brad McCoy, Dragoslav Mitic, Michael Mychajlyszyn, Jack Nairn, John Ngan, Daphne Nicolas, Mackenzie Nixon, Bas Olsman, Natalina Percival, Jozef Pavlik, Shabbar Raza, John Roddick, Erik Roth, Natalie Russell, Christian Schimert, Joel Shane, Patrick Sheaffer, Shirley Shen, Ji-Young Soulliere, Srinidhi Sridhar, Frank Stebner, Ly Tang, Arnold Wong, Iris Woo, Cedric Yu, Jinyong Yum

Support Staff Alexis Mitchell, Andrea Smith, Sydney Gelfer, Patty Zheng, Nicolette Williams, Sarah Oxland, Joyce Shen, Siobhane Galloway

The Canada Council for the Arts has been there for all of our books with funding and encouragement. Canada is a better place because of this important institution.

HENRIQUEZ PARTNERS ARCHITECTS
NEW OFFICE AT TELUS GARDEN

HENRIQUEZ PARTNERS ARCHITECTS
NEW OFFICE AT TELUS GARDEN